W9-AGL-548

MERCY *at* MIDNIGHT

LOIS
HOADLEY
DICK

MERCY *at* MIDNIGHT

*H*OW ONE
COURAGEOUS
WOMAN SET
PRISONERS
FREE

MOODY PRESS
CHICAGO

© 2002 by
LOIS HOADLEY DICK

All rights reserved. No part of this book may be reproduced in any form without permission in writing from the publisher, except in the case of brief quotations embodied in critical articles or reviews.

Library of Congress Cataloging-in-Publication Data

Dick, Lois Hoadley.
  Mercy at midnight : how one courageous woman set prisoners free / Lois Hoadley Dick.
     p. cm.
  Summary: In the late nineteenth century, a Finnish baroness's Christian faith draws her to fight for improved treatment of prisoners and her nation's freedom from tyrannical Russian rule.
  Includes bibliographical references (p.).
  ISBN 0-8024-2647-6
   1. Wrede, Mathilda, 1864-1928--Juvenile fiction. [1. Wrede, Mathilda, 1864-1928--Fiction. 2. Reformers--Fiction. 3. Christian life--Fiction. 4. Finland--History, 1809-1917--Fiction. 5. Finland--History--Revolution, 1917-1918--Fiction.] 1. Title.

PZ7.D5497 Me 2002
[Fic]--dc21

2002024432

1 3 5 7 9 10 8 6 4 2

Printed in the United States of America

Dedicated to my son
David Edward Dick

CONTENTS

PROLOGUE

It was "pea soup day" in Sornas Prison, Finland, but one young prisoner would miss the treat. This man lay in the punishment cell, chained to the stone wall by an iron collar around his neck, shouting curses and insults. When the pea soup was offered, he dashed the bowl of hot liquid into the warden's face. As punishment, his cell was not cleaned for three days. The smell of filth was unbearable. Every day, the prisoner's ranting grew louder.

Matilda Wrede heard the commotion as she passed through the corridor and asked permission to visit the man.

"You cannot go in there, Miss," the warden said. "He raves like a mad dog. The floor is awash in foulness. A refined young woman such as yourself—"

"If he is forced to live in that miserable cell," Matilda interrupted, "surely I can put up with it for fifteen minutes."

The young baroness had her way.

"Why do you treat me like a human being?" asked the embarrassed fellow as the young lady stood before him. "Nobody else does."

"Deep down in your soul I see something fine. Others would see it, too, if only you would allow it to rise to the surface."

Her words calmed him. "I have such a longing for a good person to kneel down and pray for me."

Matilda glanced at the revolting mess on the stone floor. The stench made her eyes and nose water. She feared her stomach would heave. She was wearing a new dress of blue wool, with a long skirt. It wasn't often she had a new dress, since she had embraced poverty for the sake of the prisoners and such dresses were quite expensive. This one would have to last for many years.

She sent up a quick prayer to her heavenly Father. *Oh, Lord, please take care of my dress.* Kneeling down in the muck, she prayed for the prisoner's soul.

When she rose to her feet, there was not a single stain on her dress.

1

LEG IRONS

Young Matilda Wrede stood in an open balcony window on the second floor of her home, the governor's mansion in Vasa, Finland. The seven-year-old daughter of Baron Carl Gustav Wrede surveyed the beautiful garden encircling the house. Beyond the garden, spread out before her, lay the seaport town on the Bay of Bothnia, facing Sweden. The calendar on her father's desk proclaimed the year to be 1871.

Every midday Matilda stood on one of the Finnish-style balconies overlooking the town. She particularly enjoyed watching the blacksmith who worked on a little side street nearby. Her own pony, Star, was to be shod today.

The blacksmith worked outdoors at his forge, since the weather was mild. Sweat dripped down the bulging muscles of his hairy arms. Red and blue flames from the forge sprinted up into the air.

"With spring come buds and blooms," the blacksmith sang in a truly awful roar. Like every Finn, he loved music and punctuated his movements in song. He reached into the fire with tongs and grasped a red-hot horseshoe. Clang! Clang! The sharp, familiar sound always gave Matilda a shiver of pleasure. She adored horses.

The man laid the horseshoe on an anvil and beat it into shape, just the proper size so the trembling horse nearby would never know the pain of a sharp pebble or sliver of glass in his foot.

"Helena," Matilda called her older sister. "Come and see." Helena was the only mother Matilda had ever known. Baroness Eleanora had died seven years ago when Matilda, the youngest of nine Wrede children, was only nine months old.

Helena didn't answer. Matilda knew she must be busy in her beloved kitchen. *Perhaps she's making a nice salmon pie for our lunch,* she thought. *And fruit soup from the dried apricots and pears in the pantry.*

Helena had her own private kitchen on the second floor. In the basement, the cook reigned over a huge kitchen and prepared meals for the hired hands.

A commotion on the street pulled Matilda's attention back to the town. Two men burst around a corner of the blacksmith's shop dragging a third man, a prisoner dressed in dirty gray pants and a dirty gray shirt. One warden threw the convict down next to the blacksmith's forge. The other rolled up the man's right pant leg.

The blacksmith grinned. "With spring come sun and laughter," he brayed. Using the tongs he lifted a red-hot iron ring from the fire, then welded it closed around the prisoner's ankle. Clang! Clang! The searing metal almost touched the wretched man's skin.

Matilda leaned far out of the balcony window. "No! Stop," she shrieked. "Please, please stop!" Her red hair ribbon loosened and floated downward like a stream of blood.

The prisoner's shackled leg began to redden and blister from the heat of the iron.

"Helena," Matilda screamed. "Make them stop. Helena!"

Her sister ran into the room, slammed down the window, and closed the drapes. "What a thing for a child to see. I must ask Father not to let them bring convicts to the forge anymore. My darling, come and practice your piano lessons. Forget what you saw."

Helena hugged Matilda until she was calm, then sat in a nearby chair and picked up her embroidery basket. Matilda's twenty-four-year-old sister had never married, and Matilda often wondered if it was because of her. She also wondered if Helena ever wished for her own home and a husband and babies. But she never asked.

Matilda sat on the piano bench, her back turned to the balcony window. She would never watch the forge again. She must ask Father to send Star to another blacksmith. She didn't want her pony touched by a man who could do such a cruel thing to another human being.

Matilda watched her sister sort out her colored threads. "It must be terrible for a prisoner to be locked up. Never see the sunshine. Never ski on the slopes. Never hike in the fields or wade in a meadow stream. Why must wardens also put leg irons on them?"

Helena hesitated. "The prisoners are very wicked men," she said. "Some have robbed elderly folk. Others have murdered helpless people. They must be punished. They cannot be free to enjoy life after committing such violent crimes. They are wicked men who would hurt others if allowed out."

"Surely the prison doors are locked tightly so the prisoners cannot run away," Matilda persisted. "Isn't that punishment enough?"

"Tilda dear, you must not let this upset you so. Come now, let's have no more talk of prisoners."

"But couldn't—"

"Matilda!" Helena gave a stern look.

Matilda sighed and watched her sister embroider for a few moments. Then she wandered out of the room, through the back door, and into the garden. Her black sheepdog, Ralf, raced up to her, barking for attention. After stroking him until he settled down, Matilda climbed into her favorite seat, a sturdy low branch in an old gnarled tree. It felt as comfortable as a mother's lap. Floppy leaves covered her from head to toe. The sun warmed her like a sauna.

She dug into her apron pocket and pulled out the orange she had tucked away there for an afternoon snack. "My little farm," she said, staring at the orange. Then she closed her eyes and imagined the charming, delightful farm she knew she would have some day, when she was all grown up. *I shall never, ever use convict labor from the prison,* she vowed. *If I must, I shall pay them well.* She opened her eyes and spoke to the little orange. "Now, where was I yesterday? Oh, yes. I planted potatoes on the southern slope near the flower beds." She braced the back of her head against the tree trunk. "Down by the creek I will have an adorable little bridge, and nobody will be allowed to fish there. I will sit on the bank with my toes in the water and feed the crayfish all day long."

Every day, fine weather or foul, Matilda dreamed about her little farm. In cold weather, she woke early in the morning to linger under the goose-down quilt and spend a happy half-hour managing it.

"I'll have three horses," she said. "Two for pulling the plow and one for me to ride. My horse will never have to work. He will be shod by a blacksmith who is gentle and kind, especially to human beings." She looked down at Ralf, curled comfortably among the roots of the tree. "Four dogs should be enough," she decided. "But I love dogs so, six would not be too many, I guess. And lots of cats for the house and barn."

In the distance Matilda saw the park her father had recently decided to have built. Thirty convicts worked hard clearing paths and planting shrubs. Matilda had often seen them out there, dragging their leg irons, but never dreamed how the irons were fastened on. The awful scene in the blacksmith's shop returned, multiplied thirty times. Her stomach tightened. She squeezed her eyes shut and pressed her palms into them to try to erase the hideous image.

She must do something to help. She couldn't just sit

and watch. She noticed the closest prisoner trimming a hedge near the garden. An armed warden stood at the far corner of the park with his back turned.

Matilda slid out of the tree seat and approached the convict, keeping the hedge between them. Grasping the orange tightly, she poked her hand through the leaves. The prisoner jerked back in alarm.

"Eat it quickly," Matilda whispered, her voice shaking. "He isn't looking. I'll watch. Quick!"

Through the hedge, she saw the prisoner's dirt-caked hands tear the orange to pieces. He gulped it down, rind and all, gobbling at his fingers. "Oranges," he mumbled. "I forgot how good they be. Gimme another."

Matilda fled back to the house. To think that a man must go without oranges. Without strawberries, too, she guessed. Or pears. Maybe he didn't ever get desserts.

That evening, after supper, when Helena wasn't looking, Matilda wrapped her prune tart in a linen napkin and stuffed it into her apron pocket.

Once in her room, she hung her apron over a chair and covered it with a shawl so Helena wouldn't smell the pastry. She felt light-headed and happy. An idea had unfolded in her mind like an umbrella. She wasn't sure how she would manage it, but somehow, she decided, she would feed the convicts.

As Matilda lay in her bed trying to figure out how to make the plan work, Helena appeared in the doorway. "Tilda dear, may I borrow your—" Sniffing the air, she asked, "Is that prune tart I smell?" As Matilda watched in horror, Helena followed her nose to the chair and picked up the shawl. With creased brow, she searched the apron pockets and pulled out the pastry. "Why, my dear sister," she cried, staring at Matilda, "why on earth do you have a prune tart in your room?"

"Oh, Helena," Matilda said, hopping out of bed, "I have had the most splendid idea. You know, the prisoners who are working on Father's park—"

"What about the prisoners?" Father's voice boomed from the open doorway. Matilda looked at him. His gaze moved from her startled face to the tart in Helena's palm.

"Oh, Father, the convicts are so hungry, and we have so much. Surely, we could share some of what we have."

"According to the Russian law under which we live," Father explained, "no one may aid a prisoner. You could get the convicts in trouble, too, for they are not allowed to speak to citizens or accept anything from them."

Matilda hung her head. "Yes, Father," she said, knowing there was no use pursuing the matter.

Father and Helena hugged her, then left the room, Helena taking the prune tart with her. Matilda crawled back into bed, but she couldn't sleep. Far away, she thought she could still hear the "Clang! Clang!" of the blacksmith's awful hammer.

2

HIGH WALLS

Matilda slumped on the padded bench in front of her dressing table. Today was supposed to have been a happy day for her. She'd been ill on her eighth birthday the previous March, so Pappa and Helena had promised a special celebration exactly two months later, on May 8. But as she studied her face in the carved antique mirror, her cheeks sagged like dumplings in stew.

Helena burst into the room and gave her a kiss on the forehead. "Aren't you excited about your belated birthday?" she asked. "Don't you long to know what Pappa will give you?"

Matilda stared in gloom at her reflection. "I'll never be beautiful, will I?"

"My darling, you are beautiful now."

Helena almost suffocated her with kisses. "What dreadful thoughts to have on your special day. You little goose, what's troubling you?"

"My hair is so bleached from the sun it's almost white. I have bright red patches on my cheeks. And my nose is too long."

"I'm afraid we can't do anything about that," said Helena. "You do have Pappa's nose and his steely-blue eyes. But we can change your hairstyle." She swept a handful of Matilda's pale hair over her forehead and snipped at it with her embroidery scissors. She pulled the rest of it back and anchored it on top of her sister's head with a silver barrette. "There. Those lovely thick bangs give you an older-girl look. What do you say to that?"

"Thank you," Matilda said dutifully, but she couldn't force a smile.

She heard Pappa tramping upstairs, flicking his cane at the carved railings and whistling cheerfully. At the sound of a thud on the landing, she knew he had dropped his umbrella into the holder made of a large elk horn.

"Happy birthday, daughter." Pappa kissed her on both cheeks. "I must put in a half-day at the office, then we'll go hear the birds sing at Sandviken Bay. The cook has promised to pack baskets of cold sandwiches, birthday cake, and the most delicious raspberry drink. Claims she invented it herself. Your brothers will meet us there with their families. We'll feast, you can play on the sandy beach, and Helena will sit in the shade and knit."

Matilda looked at Pappa's reflection in her mirror. He was taller than most Finns, and his hair and beard were touched with silver. He had a high forehead and a deep wave of hair over his left eyebrow. As she looked back at herself, she saw there certainly was a resemblance. *Especially the nose,* she thought mournfully.

"Now, while I'm gone, you must finish your history lesson," he said.

"Yes, Pappa," Matilda replied.

He kissed her again and stomped back down the stairs.

Matilda followed Helena to the library, where she sat at the heavy wooden table with a lamp made of lavender-stained glass. She read about the Crusades of the twelfth and thirteenth centuries, when Finland was ruled by Swedish kings. Russia had risen to power in 1809, just sixty-three years ago. Under the rule of Czar Alexander II, Finland now had her own railroads, post offices, and money. Finns were allowed to travel all over the Russian Empire and hold jobs in almost any career they chose. But Matilda chafed at the thought that her beloved country had been governed by other rulers for such a long time.

"Finland has been like a bone two dogs fight over," she said loudly, glaring at her textbook. "God does not want Finns to be Swedish. He does not want Finns to be Russian. He wants Finns to be Finns."

"Shush." Helena looked over her shoulder. "Don't take God's name in vain. You do not know what His wishes are. And you don't know anything about politics. Finland has a pleasant life as a Grand Duchy of Russia."

It's not the same as being free, Matilda thought. *We're not much better than convicts in a prison.*

The thought dampened her spirits further. She wondered

if the prisoners knew they lived under Russian rule, or if they even cared.

When the sun reached its most dazzling brilliance, Matilda heard a horse's whinny. Her father's carriage had arrived! She ran down to the back entrance, stopping at the kitchen long enough to grab a handful of carrots and apples.

"We're celebrating my birthday today," she told the two carriage horses, handing out the treats. When she returned from the picnic, Star would celebrate along with her. She would weave him a garland of flowers from Sandviken Bay, then lead him to his own low table where he would enjoy a large loaf of the round rye bread with the hole in the middle.

Pappa held open the carriage door. "Come along," he said. "I'm as hungry as a starving prisoner." When he realized the blunder he'd made, he coughed and cleared his throat.

"Pappa," Matilda said, pausing at the carriage door, "will we pass the prison on our way to the picnic?"

"Yes," her father said. "But you will not see the convicts. The walls are high. No one looks in, no one looks out."

"Oh, Pappa, I cannot bear to see the prison, knowing I am going to a picnic while they are locked away from the trees and the birds and the sunshine."

Her father gazed at her for a long moment. "Very well," he said finally. "Have one of the servants drive you in the other carriage. He can take the longer route."

"Thank you, Pappa." Matilda hugged his neck, tears dropping onto his coat.

They all met at Sandviken Bay, though Matilda was a half-hour late. After the picnic lunch, she opened her notebook and started looking for new birds to sketch. She spotted a rose finch, a sedge warbler, and a yellow wagtail.

The sky was so glass-blue it looked ready to crack open. Tree branches were crowded with feathery friends. Bird calls and trills overlapped. They sounded sweeter than violin music, like tinkling triple notes at the top of the piano scales. Matilda was glad that most Finns were avid bird watchers.

"Once I saw forty whooper swans fly overhead," her father said. "They come down from Lapland by the hundreds. They have long, snowy-white necks and black bills with bright gold tips on the ends. In flight, they look like they're swimming lazily through water."

Matilda waited eagerly for her "surprise," the birthday gift always given after the special meal and the cake. She waited and waited. No surprise. No presents. What did it mean? Was Pappa angry at her because of her outspoken ways?

She wondered all the way home. When they arrived, she went straight to her room to sulk. Pappa and Helena followed.

When she threw open her door, she saw a fairyland. All the dark wooden furniture had been replaced by white pieces, delicately carved. Pink curtains added to the enchantment. "It's lovely," she cried. "Thank you, Pappa. Thank you, Helena. I feel just like a princess."

"Even in darkest winter, you will live in springtime," said Helena.

Matilda crawled under the new pink comforter.

"Good night," said Pappa, smiling as he closed her door.

She gazed at her fantasy world with a sense of awe and wonder. But something about it niggled at the back of her mind. Suddenly it hit her. Her beautiful, new furniture had been made by convicts.

Matilda lay awake for hours.

3

THE SILENCE
OF THE PRISON

That summer, as every summer, Matilda and her family and the servants moved to Rabbelugn, by the Kymmene River in southern Finland. Rabbelugn had been the site of the Wrede estate dating back to ancient times. The first thing Matilda did upon arrival was run out to the stables and make sure her pony, Star, and the horses were comfortable.

Pekka, the stable master's son, greeted her. "Welcome back, Miss Matilda," he said, his serious brown eyes studying her. "I hope you have been well."

Pekka was two years older than Matilda and a few inches taller. He could speak Swedish and Finnish, and he knew all about horses. Pappa made sure Pekka attended both the Finnish folk school and the Swedish public school. Matilda had attended the Finnish folk school one year too. She enjoyed walking to school with the children of the farm workers, wearing the same red-and-black striped skirt, white blouse, red apron, and square leather purse they did. Carrying a knapsack with an apple and a slab of soft cheese in a crusty roll made her feel just like the other children.

"I am fine, Pekka, thank you," she said. "Will you saddle Star for me and one of the horses for yourself? I'd like to explore along the river like I did last year."

"Yes, Miss."

As they rode, Matilda soaked in the beauty of the green countryside. She waved to the foresters poling huge rafts of logs down the river to the gulf. "I've always loved this place," she said. "Do you remember when I first stayed at Rabbelugn?"

"That summer you took your new doll and tied a string around its neck. Then you dangled it in the river, teaching it to swim," Pekka said shyly. "Did you dry it out when you got back to Vasa?'

Matilda shrugged. "I don't know what happened to her. I had little interest in dolls. I've always loved animals more, especially horses and dogs."

The horse and pony trotted along the river bank, then Pekka guided them up a little hill to where the moor began.

"Race you to that big rock," Matilda shouted and pressed her heels into Star's flank. The pony responded instantly, galloping through the peaty underbrush. Matilda felt free, as if she had shaken off heavy chains.

As always, Pekka won the race. While he waited for her to catch up, he unrolled a tattered cotton tablecloth onto a flat rock and spread out their snack—a loaf of brown bread, a slab of butter, some cheese, and a bottle of brown fruit drink.

"A no-fuss banquet, just what I like." Matilda dismounted and sat in the grass, then reached for the juice. She took a sip of the cool, sweet nectar and handed the bottle back to Pekka. "Is this made from currants?" she asked.

"It is, Miss. My sister got the recipe from a woman who works at an elegant restaurant in Helsinki."

"Have you ever been to Helsinki?" Matilda asked, smearing butter on a chunk of bread.

"Once, with my father. He was on business. All I remember is the dark prison we passed with its thick stone walls."

Prison. Suddenly Matilda found it hard to swallow her bread and cheese. She tried washing it down with the fruit drink, but now it seemed warm and sour. She looked at Pekka. "Tell me about the prison," she asked, almost afraid of the answer.

Pekka shrugged. "What do you want to know?"

"Are the convicts allowed out to attend church?"

Pekka's eyebrows climbed up into his hairline. "Oh, no, Miss Matilda. Convicts never go out, except the ones who aren't too dangerous. A few work outdoors and even get a little pay. But none of them are allowed inside a church."

"Then how do they learn about God? They have souls the same as we do. Does anybody care about them?"

"They have their own chapel in the prison, Miss. They are required to attend every Sunday without fail. The clergyman flays them, he does. Preaches loud and long to remind them they are wicked sinners."

"Do they just sit and listen quietly?"

"Yes, indeed, Miss. They may not speak nor make a sound." Pekka smacked his lips as he finished the last bite of bread.

Matilda wiped her hands on the tablecloth and shook out the crumbs for the birds. "Do the prisoners have anyone to talk to?" she asked. "Do they ever have visitors?"

Pekka squinted his eyes against the sun. "What would a prisoner have to say to a visitor? These men are not educated. They would be embarrassed to talk to gentry. Besides, prisoners speak mostly Finnish."

Matilda rolled the tablecloth into a ball and handed it to Pekka. "So they talk only to each other?"

"Oh, no, Miss." Pekka shook his head. "Silence is the rule in all the prisons."

"How dreadful."

"You mustn't think such things. These are bad people. Born bad."

As she watched Pekka untether the horse and pony, Matilda tried to imagine what it would be like not to be able to go to Pappa or Helena or the servants anytime she wanted, to talk or ask questions. *What if I had nobody—nobody at all—who would listen when I needed to talk?*

"Shall we go back now, Miss?" Pekka asked, handing her Star's reins. "I saw a crate of new books arrive for you yesterday."

Books! Matilda loved reading about the lives of famous people, folk tales from other lands, histories of wars, and amazing discoveries. She raced home, as eager to see the treasures her father had brought her as she was to escape the nightmarish images of the silent prisoners.

Matilda spent hours unpacking the books and thanking Pappa for them. Where to begin? She wanted to read them all at once. She sampled a few before retiring for the night.

The next morning, Matilda made a decision. If prisoners couldn't attend church, she wouldn't either.

After Sunday breakfast, she quietly returned to her room. She sat on her bed and stared at the wall, turning over in her mind the unfairness of life.

Helena hurried by her door, then ran back. "Tilda! Why are you still in your nightgown? Hurry, now, or we shall be late for church."

"I'm not going," Matilda stated flatly. "I don't like God. I don't want to sit and listen to sermons about Him."

"Not like God?" Helena's hand flew to her open mouth. "Matilda! What on earth? Pappa!" She flew down the steps to the living room.

Matilda heard her father stomp upstairs, flicking his cane along the railings. He stood in the doorway, dressed in black with a white scarf at his neck, peering at her. Helena hovered behind his shoulder.

"I don't like God," Matilda burst out. "He allowed His Son to be killed. You would never do that, Pappa. So you are better than Jesus' Father. I like Jesus, but I don't like God."

Father gazed at her, his brow knotted. "Um-hmm," he said, then thumped back downstairs, calling Helena to follow.

Matilda spent the entire day curled up in a big leather chair in the library, reading one of her new books. That night, after supper, she returned to the chair and wrapped herself in a heavy maroon drape. The delicious meal and the warm fire soon made Matilda sleepy. She was just beginning to drift off when she heard her father and sister come in. They sat on the far side of the wide room.

"It's time," Pappa said. "I must send Matilda to the boarding school in Fredrikshamn."

Boarding school? Matilda wondered, keeping very still to make sure her presence remained unnoticed.

"Oh, Pappa," Helena wailed.

"It is a very advanced school, my dear. The girls there study the same things boys do: chemistry, zoology, astronomy, mathematics."

"But she's just a little girl," Helena protested. "Please don't send her away yet."

"My mind is made up. Matilda is obsessed with the problems of the prisoners, which she doesn't understand, and so she is angry at God. This move will take her away from Vasa and, hopefully, quell her concerns."

Helena sniffed. "I know it would be good for her to be around other girls her age. She's much too serious. But, oh, I will miss her."

Matilda shrank down into the leather chair as she listened to her father and sister leave the room. She remained there until the night candles were lit and Helena came looking for her. She never let on that she had overheard the conversation concerning her.

At summer's end, Matilda moved to the boarding school without complaint. Pappa said it was good for her, so she would suffer for his sake.

Matilda kept to herself at Fredrikshamn and made only one friend: a baby squirrel that slept in her apron pocket. The other girls didn't understand her, and they left her alone.

The teachers at Fredrikshamn were kind. They even allowed Matilda's pet squirrel to perch on her shoulder while she recited her lessons and used the metal-tipped pointer to locate the countries of the world on the wall map.

When the long, unhappy school year finally ended, Matilda returned to her home in Vasa with great joy.

Helena greeted her with a long, tight hug, then drew back to inspect her. "Tilda, darling, you're so thin. Haven't you been eating? I know the school serves nourishing meals. Have you been ill?"

"Just homesick," Matilda said, drawing her sister into another embrace. "But I do feel tired."

"Did you like the school?" Helena asked as they climbed the stairs to Matilda's room.

"I would rather be here," she admitted. "But if Pappa wishes me to go back there next year, I will obey."

Matilda slept soundly in her own bed with the pretty pink comforter, surrounded by her carved white furniture, feeling like a princess once again.

Pappa said nothing more about her returning to the school in Fredrikshamn.

4

PRISON
DOORS OPEN

When Matilda was a young teen, she attended a reception in the state ballroom wearing a long-sleeved blouse embroidered in gold and a narrow, black velvet skirt. Her pale hair poured down her back. Jewelry lay scattered over her like hailstones. Baron Wrede wanted society to notice that his daughter was now a young lady.

Some men of science were scheduled to receive awards that evening, and Matilda's father was master of ceremonies.

Anna-Lisa and Irma Jensen teetered toward Matilda in high heels, giggling behind their fans. "Tilda," the sisters called, claiming her hands.

"Where have you been hiding the past few years?" Irma asked.

"I've been ill," Matilda explained. "I stayed at home in Vasa, studying with a tutor. It's wonderful seeing so many of my old friends again."

Anna-Lisa gave her a quick kiss on the cheek. "Isn't this exciting? We've come out into society. Who knows what may happen next?"

Irma grinned. "Young men, dances, offers of marriage. Personally, I don't believe my sister is ready. She can't even make a cabbage pie without burning the crust."

"I shall marry a man of means," retorted Anna-Lisa with her nose in the air. "No cabbage pies for me." She lowered her voice to a whisper. "Tilda, a friend of my aunt's said she saw you at a revival meeting last week. Is it true?"

"Yes," Matilda replied. "An evangelist preached a sermon on John 3:16. It was wonderful."

"Did the audience jump up and down and go into hysterics?" Irma asked. "Was it awfully funny?"

Anna-Lisa steered them toward the table of appetizers. "Tilda, have you tasted the caviar and sour cream? Oh, and the smoked reindeer and little meatballs are simply delicious."

Irma pinched her sister's arm. "Bad manners to go back three times," she hissed. "Now, behave and let Tilda talk." She turned her attention back to Matilda. "I've never met an evangelist before. What was he like?"

"They say he's from Sweden," interrupted Anna-Lisa. "A handsome young man, too, I hear. And single. Did you flirt with him, Tilda?"

"Of course not."

Irma waved to a group across the room. They waved

back and joined them. The boys, starched to the ears, bowed from the waist to each girl.

"Matilda Wrede," one of the boys exclaimed. "A long time since school days, eh?"

"Tilda went to some kind of revival meeting," Anna-Lisa said. "She was just going to tell us about it. Go on, Tilda. You've always been a good storyteller."

Matilda felt her palms dampen. A strangle of words caught in her throat. "Well," she managed, "the people weren't all dressed up like they are tonight."

"Riff-raff," a boy snarled. "My father says the poor folk enjoy that sort of emotional meeting. It's their only entertainment, after all."

"The evangelist said that God . . . that God loved . . ." Matilda stumbled over the words.

"Yes, yes," Anna-Lisa said, rolling her eyes. "God loves the whole world."

"It's true," Matilda continued. "But more than that. God loves me—Matilda Wrede. He loved me so much He came to earth as a man and died on a cross. For me." Matilda felt her eyes tingle and she dabbed at them with her lace handkerchief. "I used to laugh at the Bible too. But I believe it now. I do."

The boys' faces turned scarlet and they stalked away, grumbling. The girls stared after them.

"Tilda," Irma said, "you look feverish. Perhaps you're still ill. You should ask your father to take you home." The snap in Irma's voice told Matilda the girl was not truly concerned for her health, but simply didn't want her to spoil the party.

Matilda looked around desperately. Where was Pappa? Ignoring the tears coursing down her cheeks, she dodged around the knots of people in the room, all laughing and eating and telling stories. When Matilda finally found her father, she begged him to take her home.

"All right," he conceded, "but I must hurry back for the ceremony."

Riding home in the carriage, Matilda wept. "I've brought shame upon you," she cried. "They must all be laughing at me."

"People don't usually talk about religion at a party," he said.

"I'm sorry, Pappa. But I had to tell them the truth. In the past I hated God. But now I know His name is love. He has forgiven me all my sins. Salvation is so great and pure. Such a high and beautiful thing. I don't know why I never saw it like this before."

Pappa took her hand and held it as they rode the rest of the way in silence.

Every day, Matilda opened her Bible and read. To her it seemed like a love letter from a beloved. *How it has changed,* she thought.

She smiled at her foolishness. *It hasn't changed. I have. I have new eyes to see and new ears to hear.* Matilda often pondered how she could ever repay the Lord for His sufferings for her. *Perhaps I could teach in the Sunday school or work with the Ladies Temperance League.*

One day, after breakfast, Matilda ran upstairs, eager to finish the Bible passage she'd been reading the night before. But when she neared her bedroom door, she received the fright of her life. A convict in a dirty, wrinkled prison uniform and heavy work boots stood in the doorway of her pink-and-white bedroom with chains around his ankles and wrists. He held a small metal file in one hand. His face was blank and hopeless.

Matilda fled back down the stairs. In the living room, she bumped into her father just as he was preparing to leave for work. "In my room," she cried, breathless. "Call for help. There's a . . . a . . ." She took in a deep breath. "A prisoner!"

Pappa tapped his cane impatiently. "I know."

"You know?"

"You complained the lock on your door was broken, didn't you? Well, that convict is fixing it."

Matilda gulped. "What shall I do? I cannot go back up there until he is finished."

"Nonsense," Pappa said. "Speak kindly to him and fetch him a cup of coffee."

"What?" Matilda cried, her eyes wide.

"He can't hurt you," Pappa assured her. "The warden is just down the hall."

Matilda leaned against the door frame. "But he's a convict."

"He is a human being," Pappa said. "Just speak in simple Swedish and whatever Finnish you remember." Then he left, closing the door behind him.

Matilda willed her feet in the direction of Helena's kitchen. She filled a large mug with hot coffee and climbed the stairs, her feet heavy and her knees wobbly.

"Good morning to you," she said in Finnish, offering the coffee with trembling hands.

"Thank you, Miss," he mumbled, accepting the mug. He blew into the cup, inhaled the rich aroma, then took a small sip.

"I have been reading the Bible," Matilda ventured, nodding at the thick book on her bed table. "Have you a Bible?"

He shook his head. "I have never had a book of my own."

"Goodness! Why not?"

"Can't read, if it please you, Miss. Never learned how."

Matilda took a moment to consider the consequences of his words. "But if you can't read, how can you get married, or join the church?"

"Can't," he said simply, then took another sip of the coffee.

"Are you from Vasa Prison?" Matilda asked.

"Yes, Miss. Eight of us sleep in a dormitory there. We work outside during the day." He placed the mug on the floor and returned to his work on the lock. "Thank you for the coffee, Miss. I haven't tasted coffee in years."

Matilda sat in her white rocker and watched him work. "Do you understand Swedish?" she asked.

"A bit," he said.

She switched to her natural tongue. "Last week I went to hear an evangelist from Sweden. He preached on John 3:16." She recited the verse slowly in Finnish. "I've always attended church. But that night, for the first time in my life, I understood that the great God in heaven loves me. And He loves you too," she rushed on. "He sent His Son, Jesus, to die for your sins. You can pray to the Father in heaven and He will hear you. He will speak to you as you read His Word, the Bible."

The prisoner looked down, an embarrassed expression on his face.

"Well," Matilda said, realizing her blunder, "I'm sure He would also speak if someone read His Word to you."

She saw interest awaken in his dull eyes. "Oh, Miss, do you think you could come and tell us prisoners about God? We all need to hear."

"I will," she said, standing. "I will come and visit next Sunday. Whom should I ask for?"

"My name is Halle, Miss," he said with a smile.

That night at supper, Matilda told Pappa and Helena her plan.

"Absolutely not," her father said, thumping his spoon down in his large bowl of raisin dumplings, the beef broth sloshing over the rim.

"Tilda!" Helena shuddered. "Visit a prison? The very idea gives me chills."

"But I promised," Matilda explained. "You always said a promise should never be broken."

"You may send him a Bible," her father replied, digging into the creamy rice pudding. "Helena, my dear, this is even better than usual."

"Thank you, Pappa. I used half cream and half milk."

"I promised to visit Halle on Sunday afternoon," Matilda said firmly. "He can't read."

Pappa helped himself to a second helping of rice pudding with fruit sauce. Then he sighed. "Very well. I will send a letter of permission to the governor of the prison. A warden must accompany you at all times. Helena will walk you there and back. Stay no more than fifteen minutes and come straight home."

"Thank you, Pappa," Matilda cried. Then she hurried upstairs to prepare for her visit to the prison.

5

NEXT WEDNESDAY
AT TEN

Matilda donned a gray wool dress and a long, gray woolen cape for her visit to Vasa Prison. Helena tilted her head, studying her. "Why such drab clothes, my dear?"

"They mustn't see *me*," Matilda explained. "They must see only Jesus."

The sisters walked the short distance to Vasa Prison in silence. Trolley cars glided down the main streets. Most people were home resting after the long church service and their heavy dinners. The dark sky sagged with unleashed snow. Matilda drew her cape more tightly around her as a nasty black wind blew from the bay.

"Storm tonight, for certain," said Helena. Her frosty breath puffed out of her mouth like an unwinding scroll. "If you want to turn back, Tilda, we could come another day."

Matilda gazed fondly at her sister. Beneath the wide brim of the bonnet Helena always wore, which hid her face from sun and wind, her skin looked like cream risen to the top of milk. Dark red-brown hair set off her lovely complexion. Helena was so beautiful. She really should have married.

"I must visit today," Matilda said. "I promised. But you need not come inside with me. There must be some sort of waiting room where you can stay."

"I certainly hope so." Helena almost dropped her handbag. "I have no intention of going to visit prisoners. I don't even want to see them. This is your stubborn notion, Matilda Wrede. I'll wait fifteen minutes, as Father said. Then you must come home with me. What if our friends should see us?"

Matilda sighed. Did no one understand?

To Helena's obvious relief, the prison did have a waiting area—a collection of wooden chairs around an iron stove. Helena stood near the heat, rubbing her hands together, as Matilda handed the warden her father's letter of permission. The burly man in the brown uniform stared at Matilda, read the letter, then stared at Matilda again. His head bobbed back and forth so much, Matilda thought it might fall off and roll across the floor into the woodpile. She started to remove her wool coat.

"You'll want to keep that on, Miss Wrede. The prison is not heated." The warden scowled. "You may visit only the room where Halle and his cellmates are kept." Matilda nodded. The warden shook his head and sighed. "Follow me."

Without a backward glance at Helena, Matilda followed the warden. A short way down the hall, he stopped in front of a bare, stone room where eight prisoners stood at attention wearing thin cotton uniforms and heavy metal leg irons. An unpainted wooden chair faced them, covered with a grimy towel. A smell that reminded her of dirty chicken coops and rotting vegetables nearly made her gag, but she controlled her reflexes.

"They must remain at attention, but you may be seated," said the warden, indicating the empty chair. "I am armed, so you needn't be afraid. The prisoners may not speak unless you ask a question."

Then I shall ask many questions, Matilda thought. *And I shall stand, as they do.* She searched the faces for Halle. "Greetings, my friend," she said, her voice trembling a little. "I am pleased to meet your friends. Are you well?"

He did not reply, either with words or gestures. She turned to the warden. "I asked a question. Why does he not answer?"

"Prisoners may speak only Finnish here, Miss," the warden said, "although a few understand some Swedish. I will interpret for you." He repeated her question in Finnish.

Halle's face lit up as he replied. Matilda understood most of his words before the warden interpreted them. "We are all glad to see you, Miss Wrede. Thank you so much for coming. I don't think any of us has ever had a visitor."

"Visitors are allowed only with permission of the governor," growled the warden.

"I can speak some Finnish," Matilda said. "Let me try speaking to you in simple, schoolgirl language. I want to tell you how my life changed when I discovered that God loved me, Matilda Wrede, and help you to see how He loves each one of you."

She stumbled over several words, and the warden gruffly corrected her many times. *I must include him in my witness,* thought Matilda. *He, too, has a soul that needs to be saved.*

Slowly, she told her audience of nine about the revival meeting, John 3:16, the peace she now had with God, and the joy that filled her life because of Jesus. As she continued speaking broken Finnish, the warden's interruptions grew fewer and almost friendly. The words poured out. She quoted all the Bible verses she could remember.

The warden touched her arm and motioned toward the clock in the hall. Matilda was surprised to find she had talked for forty-five minutes. *Poor Helena must be having worry-fits.*

Matilda smiled at the prisoners. "Would you like me to come again?"

"Yes, Miss Wrede." Their voices rang out like a single man. Then each answered spontaneously. "Please come back. We need to hear about God. Teach us the holy songs the gentry sing in church. Read to us from the Bible."

"Silence," the warden snapped.

"I'll be back Wednesday at ten o'clock in the morning," Matilda promised.

A messenger approached from the hall and whispered something to the warden. "Miss Wrede," the warden said, "your sister is in tears, asking to send word to your father that you have been harmed or are being held prisoner. Your curiosity has been satisfied, you've had your adventure. Now you must leave."

Matilda reluctantly waved good-bye to the prisoners, then returned to the waiting room. Helena was weeping bitterly into her fur muff. When she saw Matilda, she threw herself at her sister and hung on her neck. *Poor Helena,* Matilda thought. *How will she feel when I tell her I'm coming back again?.*

As they walked home, an orange singe of sunset proclaimed the end of the six hours of winter sunlight. "Even a stormy day can be beautiful when one loves God, don't you think?" Matilda asked.

"No."

Matilda shivered. "There was no heat in the prison," she said. "The convicts had nothing to keep them warm, not even a thin coat."

"I don't want to hear about the prison," Helena said. "I'm too tired now to make supper. Perhaps I'll ask Cook to bake tomatoes stuffed with creamed spinach and hard-cooked eggs on top."

"I wonder what the prisoners eat," Matilda mused.

"I declare, Tilda, do stop such talk. Convict life has nothing to do with us. You have done your good deed, now choose some other work for the Lord."

Matilda said nothing more until they arrived home, where Pappa was anxiously waiting for them. Matilda ran to hug him. "I was safe," she said. "God protected me." She decided not to mention next Wednesday at ten o'clock until she had time to pray about it.

"Well, that's over," her father said in relief. "You've been inside a prison. Now, let's get you two into the library where you can warm up at the fire with a cup of tea."

When they were all seated in comfortable, cozy chairs, and the hot tea had finally quelled their shivering, Pappa announced, "I received a letter yesterday from that Swedish evangelist, Reverend Bergqvist. You remember, Tilda, he spoke the night you . . . uh . . . had your . . . awakening. He is traveling to Laihia for another meeting and I have invited him to stay with us a few days."

"Oh, I would love to meet him in person," cried Matilda. "I owe him so much."

"Why did he write to you, Pappa?" asked Helena. "Do you know him?"

"No," Pappa said softly. "Your sister apparently signed some kind of guest book at the revival meeting, and the evangelist looked up her name and address. According to his letter, he was quite impressed by her sincerity, and he wishes to meet her family."

Matilda stared into her cup of tea. Why would an attractive, single man wish to meet her family? Surely, he was not thinking about. . . . No, he couldn't possibly mean that. They didn't even know each other.

She gulped her tea, almost burning her tongue. Most young people were engaged for years until the man could work his way up in the business world, buy a house, put some money in the bank. But a traveling evangelist would probably not need such things.

Then again, Matilda's thoughts raced, if she married a clergyman they could visit the convicts together. As a couple, all prisons would be open to them, even the maximum-security ones in the city. Why, as an evangelist's wife, she might even play piano and sing for the prisoners.

If Reverend Bergqvist was God's choice for her, Matilda decided, He would work out the details.

"Do you think he plans to court our dear Matilda?" Helena asked, a gleam in her eyes. "I still have Mother's wedding dress and I can cut it smaller. A man of God, Pappa. What an honor."

"You run ahead of me," Pappa said. "I am only being hospitable. I don't even know the man yet. He may be a religious fanatic. We'll simply have to wait and see."

Matilda felt her face flush. She wasn't sure whether she would cry or laugh.

Was this how God answered prayer? So swiftly, so appropriately? Just when she was worrying about how she would get permission to return to Vasa Prison, God Himself chose a husband for her. Of course, the marriage would not take place for a few years, but it seemed the Lord was promising her that He would make a way.

Matilda set down her tea, the rattling cup and saucer betraying her quivering hands. "Pappa, when will Reverend Bergqvist arrive?"

"Wednesday morning at ten o'clock."

Wednesday at ten! But what of her promise to Halle and his friends? Perhaps the visit could be postponed.

"Are you pleased, my daughter?"
Matilda smiled. "Oh, yes, Pappa. I'm quite pleased."

6

WED TO THE PRISON

Matilda pulled her pink goose-feather quilt up to her chin and listened to the wind moaning outside her room as night fell. "There are over two hundred names for wind in the Finnish language," her schoolmistress had said the year Matilda attended the village school. She was grateful now for her Finnish lessons and realized that even that had been planned by the Lord. She determined to study the language more so she would not need an interpreter.

The wind howled so loudly Matilda could barely hear the mournful horn of the town watchman. Every two hours he climbed up in the church tower and blew his horn to reassure the townspeople there was no sign of fire. Twelve years before Matilda was born, Vasa had burned to the ground. The horns provided a sense of peace and safety throughout the village.

After the excitement of the day, Matilda couldn't sleep. "I'll name some of the different winds," she decided. "There's hurricane wind, warm wet wind, wind with sleet, soft murmuring wind, fierce screaming wind, and wind that breaks clouds open like pillows and dumps snow feathers all over town."

Finally she fell asleep. But she was awakened suddenly by a sound even louder than the wind—the awful clank-clank of chains. She sat upright, clutching the pillow. Standing beside her bed stood a convict in body irons. His face was yellowed from melancholy and a lack of sunshine, deeply lined and full of sorrow. The iron chains cut into his neck, waist, wrists, and ankles.

He spoke clearly in Finnish and she understood perfectly. "Thousands of poor, chained prisoners sigh for freedom and peace in their souls. Speak to them of Jesus, while yet you have time."

A tree branch scratched her window and the man vanished into his own shadow. Matilda rose, lit a candle, and searched the room. The windows were still locked, her bedroom door shut. It was a dream, of course. Yet Matilda couldn't stop shaking. What did it mean? Had she dreamt of a prisoner simply because she had seen several the day before? Or did God want her to go alone to visit prisoners, without a husband or the blessing of the church?

Thousands. Her visitor had said thousands of prisoners were hungry for God's Word. Matilda curled up in the window seat and opened her Bible, praying for guidance.

Her eyes fell upon Jeremiah 1:6: "Ah, Lord God! behold, I cannot speak: for I am a child."

She lifted her eyes from the page. "Lord, that is exactly how I feel. I am not much more than a child. And I hardly speak any Finnish."

She read the next verse: "But the Lord said unto me, Say not, I am a child: for thou shalt go to all that I shall send thee, and whatsoever I command thee thou shalt speak."

Matilda closed the Bible. "Oh, Lord, this all seems so impossible. Forgive me for asking this, but could you kindly confirm this message?"

Prayerfully, she opened her Bible again. It fell to Ezekiel 3:11: "Go, get thee to them of the captivity, unto the children of thy people, and speak unto them."

Matilda gazed out the window all night, waiting for sunrise. The storm abated. The evergreens were dusted with snow.

When at last the day began to dawn, the sunlight was thin, as though it had been strained through a sieve. Matilda dressed in her warmest clothes. Instead of high-button shoes, she pulled on her Russian fur boots and her long coat. She wound a woolen scarf around her head and snatched her fur muff.

She tiptoed down the winding steps, then slipped out a side door. Ralf appeared and followed her onto the deserted streets with a confused look in his black eyes. Fog hooded the trees. The cold gnawed at her blood and tried to suck the life out of her as she hurried to the beach. The sea had not yet frozen. Ralf followed at her heels, eighty pounds of cheerful yap, taking care not to get his feet wet in the icy surf.

Matilda ran until a slight pain in her side forced her to slow down. Sitting on a rock, she talked to God. "I'm so confused. Is this what I am to do with my life? Go alone to visit prisoners? What of Reverend Bergqvist? Shall I never be wed?" No answer came from heaven, but in the brown and sullen dawn, Matilda's heart was filled with assurance of God's will for her life, as though He had trumpeted words from heaven. "I think," Matilda prayed, "from now on, I am wed to the prison. That will be my life."

Turning toward home, Matilda saw that the oil lamps in the house were not yet lit. Bustling servants arriving for work didn't recognize her in the half-light of dawn. With a pat on Ralf's head, she headed straight for her room, hoping her absence had not been noticed.

As Matilda reached the top of the steps, Helena's door opened. Still in robe and nightcap, her sister stepped out, holding a candle, and looked in horror at Matilda. "I went into your room to ask if you were warm enough, and you were gone. I noticed you had taken your warmest coat and boots and the dog. Why, Tilda, why?" Helena began to cry. "Did you go back to that awful prison? Were you sleepwalking?"

Matilda pulled her sister into the room and they sat together on the edge of the bed. "I simply took a walk along the beach."

"What if someone saw you wandering about? Oh, what have I done wrong? How have I failed you?" Helena wept. "Only yesterday you were my darling little sister, a charming, delightful child. Tilda, please tell me what's wrong."

Matilda embraced her sister. "God called me," she said simply.

"To walk on the beach in the dark?"

"No, that was my choice. God has been calling me in many ways, and tonight I finally understand what He means. He showed me in His Word what He wants me to do. With His help I will be a friend to the prisoners." She quoted the verses from Jeremiah and Ezekiel.

Helena gasped. "What will Pappa say?" The hand holding the candle shook. "How can you go to people in captivity? What of the Reverend Bergqvist? He seemed interested in you. Oh, Tilda, I beg you, think of your own happiness."

The sound of footsteps came down the hall and their father called, "Tilda! One of the servants said he saw you coming back from the beach. Can you imagine—" He broke off when he saw Matilda dressed in her heavy coat and boots. He looked at Helena, then back to Matilda. Anger darkened his face. "I heard Helena crying. How could you worry her so? Get dressed, both of you. We will talk over breakfast."

Matilda changed clothes quickly and ran downstairs. Pappa had his head inside the dumbwaiter hole cut in the wall, calling orders to the cook. "Send us up a good breakfast, please. Yes, I know it's early, but we're hungry." After the girls were seated, he said, "Not a word until I have had my breakfast and at least three cups of coffee."

The bell on the dumbwaiter rang and Matilda carried

the tray of food to the table. Helena only sipped at her coffee, but Matilda found she was famished. The brisk run in the cold air and the satisfaction of knowing God's will gave her a healthy appetite. She ate a bowl of hot oatmeal and some poached eggs with creamed mushrooms. Her father finished his open-faced sandwich of fish and vegetable salad while Helena toyed with a sliver of cardamom coffeecake.

Pappa shoved his chair back from the table and smiled kindly at Matilda. "Now, then. What were you doing to give your sister such a fright, eh? If you want to go kicksledding over the frozen sand, just tell me. I'll arrange a party. Perhaps on Wednesday, when Reverend Bergqvist arrives, we'll have a winter outing."

"Pappa, if he is coming to get better acquainted with me, I'd rather he didn't come at all," Matilda said. "I shall never marry." She related her dream, God's guidance in the Scriptures, and her conviction of His will as she walked the seashore. Helena wept quietly into her linen napkin.

"Pappa, since my conversion I feel I have a great debt to pay. Not to earn salvation, for I already have that. But a debt to tell the prisoners that they can live in daily communion with God through Jesus Christ our Lord. What else do they have, Pappa? I must be a friend to them, for they have no friends at all."

Her father sat with his head bowed and Matilda thought a tear or two shone on his glasses. "I will cancel the visit and make apologies," he said. "Matilda, dear daughter, I dare not stand in the way of someone with such convictions as you have."

Reverend Bergqvist did not visit. Matilda kept her appointment with Halle and his friends on Wednesday at ten.

TOOTHACHE!

"November 1884. To Halle, Prisoner #241, and all my friends at Vasa Prison. Greetings from Matilda Wrede, Rabbelugn in Anjala, Southern Finland."

Matilda blotted the neat Finnish words with a piece of felt. *I sound almost like St. Paul,* she thought. She sat at a square wooden table under a swaying kerosene lamp in the drawing room of the family estate. A cozy fire burned in the fifteen-foot-high fireplace. Natural wooden beams and a carved wooden floor gave the room a country feel.

"I know you must wonder why we moved so suddenly," she continued writing, "but my father decided to resign his governorship. I'm not sure why, and he avoids my questions whenever I ask about his reasons. But during that spell of mild weather last month, he ordered everything packed and moved, and here we are at the estate where we usually spend our summers. I will miss my visits with you, but I promise to come back someday. Meanwhile, we can correspond. My father has asked the prison chaplain to appoint someone to teach you all to read and write. Until then, I am sure the warden will read my letters to you. I will do my best to improve my Finnish." Matilda blotted again and held out the paper for her sister to see.

Helena set down her knitting and read the letter. "It's perfect. Your study of Finnish has definitely paid off." She handed the paper back to Matilda. "Writing to the prisoners is certain to encourage them. And wasn't it splendid of Pappa to buy you that nice writing paper and stamps? I'm so pleased you found a lovely Christian work you can perform right here at home."

Matilda would gladly write thousands of letters if that's what God chose for her to do. But she missed talking to the dear souls at Vasa Prison three times a week and watching the light from heaven open their understanding. Was letter-writing all that her service to prisoners was meant be?

Matilda turned back to her parchment. She started to describe the mansion and acreage of Rabbelugn, then crossed out the words. How could she write of home and fireside and luxury to men who lived in a cold, empty cell? She started to describe ice skating on the lake, then tore the letter into ragged bits.

Letter-writing was better than losing all contact with the prisoners, but it was a poor substitute for a visit. She almost wished she were a prisoner herself, like the Apostle Paul, so she could better reach the convicts for Christ. What an idea. Imagine, the daughter of a baron being sent to prison. But she was willing, more than willing.

She looked at Helena, who sat close to the fire knitting another sweater for a poor person in the village. Ralf lay by her side, a dark shadow poured across the floor.

Matilda took a new sheet of paper from her writing box. "Helena, are you happy?"

Helena dropped a stitch. "I will be, when the river freezes over. I can't wait to organize a skating party. Father bought skates for all the village children."

It had snowed that week, a perfect snow for skiing. The slope near the house was being packed down by servants, who skied over it several times, riding a sleigh pulled by two horses to get back up the hill. Soon the river would freeze and its icy top would provide a smooth, hard surface just right for skating.

Helena picked up her dropped stitch. "Aren't you happy here at Rabbelugn, dear?"

"If you're happy, I'm happy," Matilda said affectionately, though it wasn't absolutely true. She loved her family and all that was Rabbelugn. But she didn't fit in here anymore. Something kept calling her, though she wasn't sure what it was. Until she understood, she would try to be content with writing letters to her friends at Vasa.

Matilda closed her letter with Scripture and told the prisoners she was praying for them. Then she took the paper to Pekka and asked him to take it to the village post office immediately.

When she returned to the drawing room, she found Pappa waiting for her. He handed her a handwritten page. "Please ask Pekka to take this to the town crier right away so it can be announced tonight."

"It sounds important, Pappa," Helena said, looking up from her sweater.

"It is," he said. "Everyone in the village is invited to ski by moonlight on our slope tomorrow night. Afterward we'll serve hot cocoa and sandwiches here."

"What a wonderful idea," said Helena. "Tilda, you were not two years old when you first stood on skis. I held you up and you struggled along a bit, then toppled head-first into a snowdrift."

Matilda laughed. "I think you were born wearing skis, Helena. You never fall and you're faster than some of the men. But I've never heard of skiing after dark. How will we see?"

"City people often ski at night," Papa explained, "because they work all day. You will be surprised at how beautiful it is."

On the night of the ski-fest, over two hundred villagers arrived at Rabbelugn, toting their skis and poles over their shoulders. Pekka gallantly insisted on carrying the sisters' equipment up the hill for them.

Matilda, in a fur hat twice the size of her head, balanced on her skis at the top of the hill, gazing at the night sky lit by a million star specks. The moon seemed close enough to touch.

All along the ski slope torches flared, lighting a path for the skiers. Elderly men and women of the village, too frail to ski, held the torches high, leaning against evergreens for support. Some corners of the slope remained shadowy and mysterious, but the path fairly sparkled.

Matilda clapped her mittens together, sending showers of ice crystals into her face. "It certainly is beautiful, Helena. How good of Pappa to plan this."

The village children, thrilled to be up past bedtime, all begged Matilda to play with them. Some of the boys and girls stayed at the top and built snow sculptures. Others flew down the gentle incline, looking like red and blue birds in their colorful outfits.

Helena smiled at Matilda, then began her descent, skillfully angling her body first to the right, then to the left. Matilda took a deep breath and shoved off. She zipped down the slope, her skis propelling her faster and faster. Ice pellets stung her face. The flashing torches almost made her dizzy. Then, too soon, she reached the bottom and stopped by falling on her backside, much to the delight of the children.

Matilda and her sister sat on stumps at the foot of the hill to rest. "Tilda," asked Helena, "would you help me start a children's choir in the village church?"

"Of course. I've been neglecting the piano lately, but I can always begin again. Do you think anyone would be interested?"

Helena placed a gloved hand on her sister's arm. "All the children adore you, Matilda."

She laughed. "You receive plenty of adoration too."

The moment Helena stood, Pekka appeared, ready to carry the sisters' skis and poles back up the slope for another run.

After a few hours, Pappa rang the soup bell loaned to him by a farmer's wife. The big, round metal bell with slits was normally used to call farm hands to meals. Today, it signaled the beginning of the great feast.

A long table in the north hall was piled high with woven birch baskets filled with crusty rolls, platters of sliced cheese, mugs of hot cocoa, and dishes of pickles. The townspeople devoured the delicacies until they all claimed they couldn't possibly eat another bite.

After the last tired villager had expressed his thanks to Baron Wrede and headed home, Pappa joined his daughters in the entry hall. "Tired, my girls?"

Matilda made a pile of her wet coat and scarves for Brita, the housekeeper, to take away and dry. "Tired and sore. Oh, my legs. And my back. Even my elbows hurt."

Her father chuckled. "I already asked Brita to prepare the sauna. That will take care of your aches and pains."

"The sauna," Matilda cried. Never having gone to Rabbelugn in the winter, she'd forgotten they even had a sauna. "Can we roll in the snow afterward?"

"You can if you wish," said Helena. "I shall just sit in the cooling room."

Matilda and Helena draped themselves in long towels and entered the small wooden enclosure near the east side of the house. The wood stove filled the room with waves of heat. A pile of stones, like cannonballs, lay on top of the stove, turning white and dusty from the heat. The girls giggled as they climbed the steps to the platform over the stove.

"Fold your towels neatly and throw them down to

me," instructed Brita, a solid, middle-aged woman whose brown hair dotted with white flecks was bundled in a knot at the nape of her neck. Matilda thought it looked just like a Shrove Tuesday bun.

Setting aside the folded towels, Brita dashed a dipper of water on the white-hot stones. They hissed, sending up clouds of fine steam.

Matilda seized a bundle of birch twigs, dipped them into a pail of water, and switched them against her sister's back, then her own. The sweet smell of birch filled the air.

"More steam?" Brita called up to them.

"Yes, please," shouted Matilda. The fresh steam rose, and for one glorious moment it erased all her aches and pains. Then she felt as though her hair was on fire and her skin scalded. Sweat blinded her as she groped for the steps. "Brita! Help me!"

The housekeeper's strong arms lifted her down and wrapped her in a robe.

"Water," cried Matilda. "Snow!" She stumbled out of the sauna, knelt in the snow, and rubbed handfuls over her head and arms. She looked up to see Brita smiling down at her.

"Come with me," the housekeeper said, then she led Matilda to the cooling room, where her sister sat, quite unruffled. Brita poured cool water over Helena's shoulders.

"Dear sister," Matilda cried, "are you all right?"

She laughed. "I guess I'm more used to it than you are. Look. Doesn't my complexion seem clearer?"

"Ask Brita. I can't see with all the steam. I feel like I've been boiled alive."

"But all your aches and pains are gone, aren't they?" Helena asked with a smile.

"Indeed, they are," she agreed. "I'm sure to have a marvelous sleep tonight."

But she didn't. Matilda woke around one o'clock in the morning with a toothache that throbbed along the entire left side of her head.

8

THE CHAIN GANG

Hold still." Helena propped Matilda's mouth open and packed a cotton ball soaked in oil of cloves around the aching tooth. "This will help the pain, but you must hold your hand on your cheek to keep it warm."

Matilda obeyed. "I smell like rice pudding," she mumbled around the cotton.

"The carriage is ready." Pappa called up the steps.

Helena led her sister downstairs.

"Pekka will drive you to the railroad station," Pappa said. "The specialist in Helsinki will have that tooth out in no time. Then you and your sister can stay ten days or so to see the sights. There's a nice hotel right next to the station."

Matilda hugged him good-bye, then

Pekka and Helena helped her into the carriage. As they rode into town and boarded the small train, even the pain in her mouth couldn't spoil Matilda's excitement. She would finally see Helsinki, the capitol of Finland, a city of museums, ancient churches, stores, and restaurants.

"Hel-sinki-sinki-sinki," the steam engine seemed to chant as it chugged along, its cadence putting Matilda to sleep like a lullaby.

The offending tooth was pulled, and after a day's rest at the hotel, Matilda declared she didn't even miss it. "What a beautiful suite of rooms," she said, admiring the priceless rugs and matching drapes.

"I had only to mention Pappa's name," Helena said. "Now, if you're really up to some sightseeing, let's devote today to exploring the streets of Helsinki. Then we can shop for clothes and gifts." Her eyes sparkled. "While you were napping yesterday, I bought us tickets for the National Opera House. I also got tickets for a choral concert at the Johannes Church, the largest church in Helsinki. It's been ten years since I've been here, and there's so much I want you to see."

The day was clear and cold. When the frosty mist over South Harbor lifted, Matilda saw small ice chunks floating along the black waters of the Gulf of Finland. Oarsmen in small, heavy boats worked frantically to steer the ice away from the other boats.

"See all those docks on the waterfront?" Helena pointed. "Farmers bring potatoes, root vegetables, and fresh fish to the market year round. Those warehouses used to be the dens of smugglers and other criminals."

"What's that red-and-yellow brick building?" Matilda asked.

"That's Old Market Hall. It's an indoor market, all polished and very expensive. They have bread and reindeer cold cuts and a delicious cheese. Let's go there for lunch."

As they strolled down the lovely avenue, enticing aromas floated all around them.

"Bulevardi is one of Helsinki's finest streets," Helena explained. "There's the National Opera House, where we'll be going the day after tomorrow. Only Russian officers stationed here are supposed to attend, but—"

"I know," Matilda interrupted, laughing. "You just mentioned Pappa's name and got us two tickets."

"That is how it happened." Helena looked at her. "I suppose I should feel terribly guilty, but is there anything wrong with being wealthy? Pappa uses his money to help needy people too."

After lunching on Russian kebob, they walked through Senate Square, which held much of Finland's national history. Helsinki University covered the entire western border of the square.

"I want you to see Helsinki Cathedral," Helena said. "Can you climb steps like a goat?"

Matilda followed Helena up crumbling stone steps so steep she had to lean forward to keep her balance. The outside of the impressive cathedral was bordered by tall Corinthian columns. Statues of graceful figurines covered the rooftop.

Inside, a gold organ and a gold altar gleamed against walls painted pearly white. The noise of the street was hushed. Matilda feared to breathe lest she disturb the holy quietness.

"What do you think?" Helena whispered.

"It's like the pure and simple gospel of Christ."

Helena studied her for a moment. "You feel so deeply," she observed.

Matilda sensed a disturbance deep in her soul, as if she had forgotten something. Something important.

Helena took her arm. "Come see the three statues." They walked somberly to the far corner of the room.

"I recognize Martin Luther," Matilda said. "But who are the others?"

"Two of Luther's disciples, Philip Melanchthon and Mikael Agrikola, who gave us our Finnish New Testament."

After staring for several moments, Matilda followed Helena back down the steep stone steps to the street.

"I spied some Gypsy women yesterday," Helena said. "They sell the most exquisite lace you have ever seen. Aprons, scarves, baby blankets." She pinched Matilda's arm. "We must not go home without some baby clothes, Tilda dear."

Matilda felt her sister's arm clinging to her own. "Why?"

Helena giggled. "You know. To put by, with other things for a home, like linen and towels. You're twenty-one years old now, my dear sister. You must begin thinking about such things."

Matilda eased her arm from Helena's grasp. "That sign says this is Mannerheim Street. It looks like a main artery."

"It is," said Helena. "We'll turn right here, onto Alexander Street, and you'll see theaters, watchmaker's shops, furniture stores, and banks. Oh, isn't the city wonderful, Tilda? We should come here every month and stay a few days. Look at the gold fabric in that window. I want to buy yards and yards of it to redecorate my bedroom."

Matilda nodded, but the pleasure of the day had ended for her. She squinted up at the sky. It seemed a bit darker somehow.

At the corner of Mannerheim and Alexander Streets, people were crowding onto the sidewalk. "Are they making room for some sort of parade?" Matilda asked. Before Helena could answer, a chain gang appeared in the middle of the street. Two armed guards were beating the convicts with clubs and kicking them to make them move faster.

Anger and pity boiled up inside Matilda. She shoved and fought her way through the crowd. "Stop," she screamed. "You have no right to beat these men."

The guards stared at her fine clothes and fur cape. "Don't come any closer, Miss," one implored. "These are dangerous beasts."

"They are human beings," she retorted, looking into the men's faces. She knelt by a convict who had fallen in the icy street. His face bled and his bare hands were blue and swollen. With a gasp, she realized it was her friend from Vasa Prison. "Halle! How is it you are here?"

"Transferred, Miss Wrede," he groaned. "I got in a little trouble a month ago and was sent here to Helsinki Prison. Visit us, Miss, if you can."

"I will. I give you my word."

As the guards prodded the prisoners along, Matilda looked around for Helena, but the crowd had separated them. She retraced her steps down Mannerheim Street and bumped into her sister clinging to a policeman's arm.

"Tilda! Oh, Tilda darling. I thought those wretches had attacked you. I saw you fall onto the ground. Oh, what have they done to you, the vile creatures?"

"I'm perfectly all right," Matilda said. "Sir, could you please direct us to the office of the Chief Inspector of Prisons?"

The policeman gave her a confused look, but said nothing. He led the sisters to the office. Helena took a seat in the waiting room as Matilda approached the receptionist.

"I am the daughter of Baron Carl Wrede, governor of Vasa until a year ago. I would like a permit to visit all the prisons of Finland."

The receptionist looked at her in astonishment. "Wouldn't you feel more at home on the ballroom floor?" she snickered.

"I want to make friends with the prisoners," Matilda persisted, ignoring her comment.

"Why?" asked the dazed woman.

"So I can tell them how much God loves them."

Her eyes narrowed. "And what does Baron Wrede think of this?"

Matilda swallowed hard. "I haven't told him yet," she said honestly. "But I visited Vasa Prison with his consent all last summer."

"Best way to cure a sickness is to give a good dose of it, I always say," mumbled the receptionist.

"I beg your pardon?" Matilda asked, raising her brows.

Rolling her eyes, the receptionist called for the Chief Inspector. He was short for a Finn, with a face pink as salmon and ears fastened very close to his head. Matilda made her impassioned plea.

"I will give you the permit," he said, "and even write letters of introduction to some of the governors, if you promise me one thing."

"What is that?"

"Be sure your father knows of your plans."

"Thank you," Matilda said with relief. "I can promise that."

He signed the papers and handed them to her, and she folded them into her muff. Then she rejoined Helena in the waiting room. They took a trolley back to the hotel.

Matilda unhooked the fur cape from her winter coat and placed it in the back of the closet. Then she unpacked the plain black dress she had worn to the dentist.

"Tilda dear, what of our vacation?" Helena moaned.

"My dear sister, I won't spoil your good time. I will go wherever you want in the afternoons. But in the mornings I am going to visit the prisons of Helsinki."

A look of great sorrow spread over Helena's face.

"My dear sister," Matilda said, her heart breaking, "I would never wish to hurt you. But I must obey God."

9

GRACE AND PEACE SHALL BE MY SHIELD

Matilda wore her plain black dress with the leg-of-mutton sleeves and her coat without the fur cape. She decided against a muff, and pulled on black gloves instead.

Helena looked her over. "Well, you're plain enough. I'll shop while you're gone, but I'll worry the whole time. Tonight we'll dine at the Kappeli Restaurant on the Esplanade, and then attend the opera. Pappa asked the hotel to provide two gentleman escorts. They're second cousins of Pappa's, thrice removed. Won't that be fun?"

Matilda wasn't sure she would feel much like having fun after visiting the prison. "There is something you could do for me," she said. "I would like some sort of plain brooch to wear at my neck. I would like the words *grace and peace* inscribed on it in Finnish."

"Armo ja Rauha," Helena translated. "I will ask a jeweler to make it for you."

"Nothing expensive," Matilda said.

"Don't worry. There's plenty of money left."

"I want the prisoners to see the pin first, before they notice me. It may turn their thoughts to God. Have it made in the form of a shield. Grace and peace shall be my shield."

After hugging her sister good-bye, Matilda set out on foot for the prison. It was a small one down a narrow street near the waterfront. When she said good morning to a vendor, the air was so cold her voice cracked. She missed her fur cape.

As she handed the governor of the prison her papers of permission, the man looked at her with suspicion. He peeked out into the hall to see if anyone was with her. "I will go with you," he said. "The chaplain will accompany us, and also an armed guard." His spidery fingers traveled to and fro over her papers.

"No, thank you," Matilda said. "I am not afraid. I visited the prison in Vasa for almost a year and was allowed in the cells without anyone else present. The prisoners will not feel free to speak their mind if others are with me." The man scowled, but Matilda refused to be intimidated. "I would like to see a prisoner named Halle, who was transferred here from Vasa."

"That man's a troublemaker," he said. Matilda stood her ground. He sighed. "Follow me."

Matilda entered a dark corridor with cells on each

side, where men lay about in chains. Like turnips stored in a bin, she thought. Taking a breath was like trying to breathe underwater, the air was so damp, and heavy with bad odors. How could anyone think the convicts would be "reformed" in such conditions?

The prison governor unlocked one of the doors. "This is against my better judgment," he said. "You may call the guard when you have finished your business."

Matilda thanked him and ventured into the cell. Halle sat in irons.

"Good morning, my friend," she greeted him. "How is it with your soul?"

The man did not lift his eyes. "Ah, Miss, I am ashamed you should see me like this. Forgive me for betraying your trust. I was tempted to steal, and there is no help when a man is tempted."

"Yes, there is help. Jesus Himself is our Great High Priest who has suffered everything you suffer. He said you would not be tempted more than you are able to bear."

Halle lifted his head in wonder. "How can He help?"

"He makes a way of escape. You wrote to me that you accepted Him as your Savior. Trust Him in this also. Pray, and avoid temptation with all your might. Resist Satan and he will flee."

"Does it say that in the Bible, Miss?"

"Indeed it does." Matilda opened her small New Testament and read him First Corinthians 10:13.

"What a wonderful thing." His face creased in a smile. "Will you tell Anti, my friend next door? And Eerno across the corridor?"

"Yes, I'll visit them, too, but first let me read more to you from God's Word." Matilda chose the fourteenth chapter of John, and a psalm, then she prayed.

"God bless you, Miss Wrede. What a wonderful day this is. How glad I am to see you again."

Matilda called the guard and asked to be let into the next cell. After some hesitation, he unlocked the door.

In the dirty yellow light from a tiny window near the ceiling she saw a young man lying on a pile of straw, curled up on his side like an animal. "Good morning, Anti. My name is Matilda Wrede. Halle said you might like a visit."

He stared at her. "You look like springtime," he muttered. "Just for a minute, standing there against the light of the open door, you looked like something fresh and alive come into this filthy hole."

"Well, I am alive, and I'd like to sit down and talk to you."

"You can't sit on that dirty pallet," he protested. "I threw up on it yesterday."

"Really?" Matilda said gaily. "Well, I'll just sit here anyway." She lowered herself onto the pallet, ignoring the putrid odor wafting from it. "I bring you greetings from the great and good Father in heaven."

Anti snorted. "He doesn't care for me. Nobody cares about me."

"I do," Matilda said. "I'd like to read to you the very words God said when He was thinking of you one day." She read John 3:16.

"Is it true?"

"Absolutely. He saved a sinner like me." She waved

away his protests. "Oh, yes, I am a sinner too. I am a Wrede, and we Wredes have bad tempers and often demand our own way. I have lived a selfish life. I've not always been truthful. But God loves me, as He loves all mankind. He sent His Son, Jesus, to die for me. And for you, too, Anti.

Anti tried to move toward her, but his slight movement caused great pain from the heavy shackles. Matilda removed her silk scarf and tucked it under the iron at his neck. The skin was worn thin and bleeding.

"If the great Father is like you, Miss, then I love Him," Anti said.

Matilda felt like weeping, but knew that would only upset her new friend. She read a chapter from the New Testament, then a psalm, and prayed. "I will come again," she said, and called the guard.

Matilda visited three more prisoners, then walked back to the hotel. She found Helena waiting with a small jewelry box in her hand.

Matilda lifted the brooch and admired it. "It's lovely," she said. "Dull silver, very tasteful. *Grace and peace.* God grant I may know it each day, for I will need it." She sat on the bed and cried, unable to hold back her tears any longer.

Helena held her tightly. "My darling, you are not well. Is there no other way to help these people?"

Matilda shook her head. Worn out, she curled up on the bed and soon fell asleep. When she awoke the room was dark, the sky having grayed into dusk. Helena was laying out a light green frock with a lacy fringed shawl for her. "Are you feeling better?"

"I am hungry." Matilda brushed her hair, parting it in the middle and pulling it back. The pale blonde of childhood had turned to mousy brown.

"We'll take a carriage to the restaurant," Helena said, "so we won't get chilled."

Matilda changed into the frock and shawl. "I love the pin. Was it costly?"

Helena smiled. "Pappa will be happy to know you spent a bit of the money on yourself. I'm afraid he will chide me for buying everything I wanted."

At the Kappeli Restaurant, Helena seized upon the French menu with delight. "Do you remember your French lessons, Tilda? We can order anything we want. Do you wish to try snails?"

"Not at all. I had them once. When Pappa brought them home. They were tasty in the mouth, but afterward—ugh, how they lingered. Why don't you order for me."

After placing their order, Helena asked the blessing. "Such luxury," she said, opening her eyes. "Candlelight all around. Aren't the shadows fascinating?"

Matilda gazed around her. All that the world called beauty and refinement surrounded her. She had only to wish for something, and she knew it would be given to her.

Back at the prison, the five convicts she had seen were probably eating bowls of greasy cabbage soup. Cabbage soup was standard fare in the prisons.

A suave waiter arrived with a platter filled with a dozen kinds of hors d'oeuvres, then stood by to anticipate the women's slightest need. A young boy in a dark suit hovered among the tables with a tray full of butter pats on ice, whose only job was to refill empty bread-and-butter plates.

Matilda looked at the loaded platter of hors d'oeuvres and felt sickened. She picked up her fork and teased the asparagus. She flaked the delicate fillet and stirred it in circles.

Helena looked up, her mouth stuffed with seafood. "Is something wrong with the food?"

"I'm sorry. I can't eat. Go ahead and enjoy, I'll just sit here." She felt tears coming again. "I can't talk about it right now."

Matilda kept her eyes on the slender white candle on their table. How quickly it melted. It had burned down an inch since they arrived. The candle would soon turn into smoke and be gone forever. Life seemed just as short. And there was no bringing back a minute of it.

At Helena's request, the maître d'hôtel brought their coats. "We'll have a snack after the opera," Helena said. "Maybe you'll be hungry then."

When they returned to the hotel, Matilda felt even worse. "I can't go to the opera," she said, wincing at the annoyance in her sister's eyes. "Please go without me, Helena. I'll be all right here, and our cousins can take proper care of you."

Helena sat at the gilded dressing table. "Tilda, God ordained you to be born a baroness. Don't you think you are rebelling against Him by wishing to be something else?"

"But God called me."

"And what about the children's choir you said you'd help me start?"

"I will honor my promise to you as much as I can," Matilda said. "But I must follow what the Lord has called me to do."

Helena's shoulders slumped. "Will you stay indoors until I get back?"

Matilda nodded. "I can read or nap."

"Then I'll go. I don't want to miss the opera." Helena twirled into her fur coat, picked up her muff, and flounced off to the lobby to wait for the escorts.

10

OH, YOU
SINNERS!

Following her trip to Helsinki, Matilda kept quiet about the prisoners, afraid to stir up any opposition at home. But soon she felt a call to begin a ministry at Tavastehus, the state prison for women in Finland.

After recovering from the initial shock of her announcement, Pappa gave Matilda the address of a good boarding house near the prison and some extra money. Helena silently brushed her black dress. Matilda's "Grace and Peace" pin shone at her throat.

On the train to Tavastehus, Matilda closed her eyes and tried to nap. *Lord,* she prayed, *I'm afraid of what I'll find at Tavastehus.* She had heard that female prisoners were hard and bitter. Perhaps they would not want to hear her message. *Help me, Lord.*

Matilda walked from the train station to Tavastehus, carrying her small valise. A large courtyard surrounded the stone building. The icicles hanging from the eaves looked as beautiful as cut glass.

Entering the prison office, Matilda was met by the chief warden of the prison, a woman named Tarja. Her snapping black eyes flashed hatred as she eyed Matilda. Matilda returned her stare.

"No visiting." Tarja's eyes gauged Matilda. "However . . . I suppose I must make an exception for you, Baroness."

"Please do not mention the title. I wish only to be known as Miss Wrede."

"Oh, the humility of the gentry."

"Please go over my papers," Matilda said sternly. "If there is a problem, I will ask the Chief Inspector of Prisons in Helsinki to make an inspection trip here to see why his letter is not honored."

"Oh, we will honor the Chief Inspector's letter," Tarja said hastily, scanning Matilda's papers and handing them back. "Welcome to Tavastehus. You have arrived at chapel time. Chapel is across the hall. Please be seated wherever you like."

Matilda walked toward the small building and was relieved to see several women walking about freely, no body irons in sight. Others sat in cells with wooden doors and peep holes.

The chapel was a bare room with wooden benches and a lectern up front. Matilda made a mental note to bring a pot of flowers next time and a strip of colorful fabric for the lectern. She sat in the back row next to a blonde girl who would have been pretty had she bathed and combed her hair. She looked curiously at Matilda, her eyes as clear as water. Matilda smiled and introduced herself.

"I'm called Wendla," said the girl.

"Do you work here?" Matilda asked, thinking this fragile beauty looked about the same age as she.

"Oh, no, Miss. I'm a murderer."

Matilda reached for her hand. "I'm so sorry." What to say next? All of Matilda's memorized greetings flew out of her head. "Will you be here long?"

Wendla smiled wanly. "Yes. I killed a man. He mistreated me, but it was still wrong, of course."

The room filled up. Tarja stood at the lectern and announced the hymn. Most of the women hummed their way through it. Matilda tried to sing along. Wendla sat with her head lowered and picked at her fingers.

The visiting clergyman was a man with a square face, hands, and fingernails. His sermon was basically sound, but he was interrupted several times by the dreadful Tarja, standing in the side aisle beating a clenched fist into her palm and exclaiming, "Oh, you sinners! Oh, you sinners!"

Matilda looked at Wendla. The girl was visibly shaken, self-loathing written across her face. Her very soul seemed to frizzle down into a grease spot.

The sermon ended, and the women mumbled their way through a closing hymn. Matilda touched Wendla's shoulder. "Have you repented of the deed that brought you here?"

"Oh, yes, Miss. A thousand times."

"Do you wish for God's mercy and forgiveness?"

Tears spilled down Wendla's face. "Tarja says I cannot hope for forgiveness," she whispered. "She says we must suffer agonies of repentance. We must be punished and punished and punished. Then we may hope God will forgive us. But He never forgives murder, Tarja says."

"I have something to show you." Matilda opened her New Testament and read, "There is therefore no condemnation to them which are in Christ Jesus." She turned a few pages and read, "Whosoever shall call upon the name of the Lord shall be saved." She looked into Wendla's eyes. "Jesus' blood shed on the cross washes away sin. Any sin. All sin."

"Those verses aren't for me," Wendla said sadly.

"Whosoever means you, too, Wendla. Do you doubt God?"

"No." The haunted look left her eyes. "But are you sure, Miss? Tarja says—"

"Never mind Tarja. Wendla, will you right now in your heart invite the Savior to come in and forgive you and make you God's child?"

"I'm a murderer."

"My dear, so am I." Wendla's eyes grew large. "The Bible says if we have hated anyone we are murderers. Who has not hated? I know I have. But God has saved me. He loves you, Wendla, just as you are."

The girl took deep breaths as though she were actually drinking in the message of salvation. "God's love," she said slowly. "Oh, I do believe it, for I see you here before me, come to visit poor women who have no other friend." The frail girl embraced Matilda. "I heard Tarja call you *baroness.* Is it true?"

"It doesn't matter. Here, let me leave you a New Testament so you can learn more about the Lord."

Wendla took the Book and held it tenderly. Then she jumped up and ran toward Tarja. Matilda saw them talk and gesture. When Wendla went to speak to the clergyman, Tarja stomped across the floor to Matilda.

"Wendla is happy," she said accusingly.

"Yes, isn't it wonderful?" Matilda stood. She felt like hugging this woman.

"She's happy," Tarja repeated. "Don't you understand how long I've worked with her to make her feel her sin? And now you come and spoil it all. I've talked to that wicked creature for weeks and months to make her feel remorse. And now she's happy."

Well, here is a soul just as needy as Wendla, thought Matilda. "Tarja, can you sit down here with me for a few minutes? I would like to tell you how God saved a sinner like me." Matilda touched the woman's arm. "Please?"

Tarja threw off Matilda's hand. "You would put me into the same class as that hussy and preach to *me?*" She shot a withering look of blackest hatred, then stalked away.

I have made an enemy now.

Matilda visited Tavastehus for two more days, but didn't see the female warden again. After three days she felt utterly weary. *Oh, Lord,* she prayed as she traveled home, *help Pappa and Helena understand what I am doing. Make us of one mind.*

Her father met the train and they chatted all the way home, about everything but prisons. When she had finished a late supper, they lingered around the table.

"I have something for you," Pappa said, handing Matilda an envelope.

"Why, thank you." Matilda opened the envelope to find an official-looking document dated May 16, 1888. "What is it?"

"A pass for you to travel on any railway in Finland," her father said. "You can come and go as you wish without worrying about the fare." He took her hand. "I realize, by doing this, I am making it possible for my youngest daughter to go far away from me for long periods of time. I want you to know I understand your work on behalf of prisoners."

Helena ran around the table to hug her. "Tilda, darling, I want to do my part too. I will be your secretary. I will help you write holiday letters to prisoners and their families. Why, some day you may be writing to hundreds of people. You can write to me when you are away from home and I'll bind the letters into a book. You can keep a diary and I'll publish it for you someday."

We are still a family, Matilda thought happily. *They understand and want to help.*

She decided to tell them about Wendla and the awful Tarja.

11

THE LITTLE
FARM

Five hundred prisoners, and I am to be the chapel speaker. Matilda reread the letter from the governor of Kakola Prison as she rode the bumpy train to Abo. The man knew her father, had heard of her work with the prisons, and wrote to invite her to Kakola.

Matilda closed her eyes and laid her worry before the Lord. *Dear Father in heaven, will I remember all my Finnish? Will my knees tremble? I have never faced so many people, and all of them prisoners. Many are life-termers. Guide me with Your Spirit, so they may not see Matilda Wrede, but Jesus only.*

The huge prison sat on the hill above Abo like a crown on a king's head. The sea lay at its feet. After gazing at it from the train station for a moment, Matilda hailed a carriage.

Ten minutes later, the kindly governor was greeting her and introducing her to the chaplain.

"I certainly do appreciate your coming," the chaplain told her with a friendly smile. "I am sure the men tire of listening to me. Today, they will have a treat."

Matilda couldn't think of herself as a "treat."

The chaplain escorted her to the vestry, where she sat in a chair at the back and watched the prisoners assemble. Her heart raced wildly as hundreds of prisoners noisily took their seats. When the chaplain beckoned, she made her way to the lectern and clutched it on both sides to keep from swaying.

"Grace be unto you and peace from God our Father and from our Lord Jesus Christ," she began. The prisoners began to settle down. Matilda sensed God's presence in her soul and all fear vanished. She spoke in perfect Finnish. God seemed to choose all the right words and put them into her mouth. She had no idea how long she spoke.

As she described God's wondrous love for all, she heard sounds of weeping and groaning. She looked around at her audience. Most of the men held their heads in their hands, sobbing like children.

Hastily she closed with prayer, then returned to her seat as she had been instructed to do. The chaplain mingled with the men as they were escorted from the chapel by guards. Then he returned to her and thanked her for coming. "The men would like you to visit them in their cells," he said. "Can you stay a little longer?"

Matilda nodded. A friendly guard led her down the

long corridors and unlocked door after door. The prisoners eagerly listened to the gospel message from the Bible.

As Matilda approached one cell, the guard stopped. "This next prisoner is named Olaf. He does not attend chapel. He does nothing but sigh and brood. He used to be a banker at a prestigious firm in Helsinki, till he was arrested for swindling and cheating people. Now he's so melancholy he's up to his nose in it."

Matilda nodded, indicating that she still wanted to visit this prisoner. The guard unlocked the cell door.

"Good day, friend Olaf," Matilda began.

"No days are good to me, Miss. All I can think of are my crimes. I have done nothing but evil all my life. I have never performed a single good deed."

Matilda's eyes searched the room. There on a little shelf sat a cracked, dirty mug. It was stained—by what, she refused to dwell upon.

"I'm terribly thirsty," Matilda said. "My throat is dry from speaking in chapel. Would you have a little water in that mug?"

He laughed. "Did you come to make fun of me? I know you are the daughter of Baron Wrede. Do you really mean to drink out of that filthy mug?"

"I do, if you would be so kind."

He stared at her. Then he grabbed the mug and handed it to her.

Without looking at it, she drained the mug and gave it back. "Thank you for your kindness, Olaf."

His smile lit up his whole face. "I thank you, Miss. This is the happiest day of all my prison life."

"How long have you been here?" asked Matilda.

"Forever, it seems. This is my third arrest. Every time I get out, I try to find a job, but nobody will hire me. No man trusts me. So I end up going back to what I do best—cheating and swindling."

Noticing the time, Matilda said, "I must go now, but I will leave you this little New Testament." She pulled the small Book from her pocket and handed it to him. "I hope to come again. Then we can discuss how my friend Jesus can change your life."

After bidding good-bye to the chaplain, Matilda hailed a carriage. "The train station, please," she said to the driver, who was so bundled in scarves that only the tip of his nose and his eyes showed.

Riding back to Rabbelugn on the train, Matilda put her concern before the Lord. *Father, what can be done to help ex-convicts?*

Her family welcomed her home, eager to hear of her experiences. Matilda told them about her visit. Then she rested for a few days, allowing Helena to wait on her.

One cold February evening, Pappa approached the girls in the library and said, "How would you like to take a short walk with me along the Kymmene River? The moon is out."

Matilda checked the thermometer on the outside of the window. Ten degrees below zero. "We must dress warm," she said. "Helena, may I borrow a scarf?"

Her sister stared at her. "You own three dozen wool scarves. Will none of them do?"

"I gave them all to the prisoners," Matilda said quietly.

Helena shook her head as Pappa led them out the back door and down the path. Ralf tagged along, nosing into all the snow drifts, hoping for a rabbit. Pekka carried a lantern and went before them on the road.

"Night has put on all her jewels," Pappa said, looking up into the dark sky. The girls laughed. Their father was rarely poetic, but it was a winking-star night, still and clear with no hint of wind. Pine and spruce trees, furred with snow, lined their path.

They walked to the Tuomenoja farm, which had been deserted for years. The barns were still in good condition. Hundreds of fruit trees surrounded the barns, waiting for spring to release their buds. Pappa stopped, called Pekka to come closer with the lantern, and took a bulky envelope out of his coat. He handed the envelope to Matilda, and she opened it curiously. Inside was a stack of papers with her name on them, all stamped with government seals.

"Tilda, my dear, that is the deed to this farm. I purchased it for you. I think it would make a fine home for ex-convicts. They could work the farm until they can make their own way in the world. I think it will bring hope and courage to your poor friends. Perhaps your brother Hendrik can run it for you when he returns from Russia in the spring."

My little farm. She had never told Pappa about her childish fantasy. And yet her dream had come true.

The moment she returned home, Matilda began to plan it on paper. She named the farm Toivola—the Wood of Hope. She and Helena wrote letters to all the governors of prisons in Finland, telling of her plan to employ ex-convicts. By spring, she had the names of thirty prisoners due to be released who would gladly work for Matilda Wrede.

That spring, as soon as the ground could be plowed, her father hired gardeners, builders, a cook, and kitchen workers. "These are only temporary," he said. "Your prisoner friends will learn to cook, plant, and take care of the livestock."

With Pappa's and Hendrik's help, Matilda's farm was soon filled with ex-convicts. But Matilda found supervising prisoners far more difficult than visiting them. The men grew accustomed to her kindness and started taking advantage of her. They seemed to think she would not notice if they were lazy or careless.

One morning, when her father and Hendrik were in town purchasing supplies, Matilda stood in the small room she used for an office and looked out the window. "I'm getting nowhere," she said to Ralf, who always listened with both ears. "The men must learn that I expect them to work hard and obey me. Hannu has spilled the paint can three times, and has only half-painted the fence. I shall have to take him to task about it."

She stepped outside the farmhouse and called to Hannu, who had given up on the fence and started attempting to split kindling. "Hannu," Matilda said in her sternest voice, pointing at the fence, "you must finish the painting job you were assigned."

Before she could say anything further, Hannu rushed at her, the ax held high.

Matilda forced herself not to budge. "Put the ax down

this minute," she snapped. Surprisingly, he did. "I want to see you in my office," she added.

She stormed into the small room. She sat at her desk and waited. Thirty minutes passed.

Finally, out of the corner of her eye, she saw Hannu appear in the doorway. To hide her shaking hands, she laid a pad of paper on her lap and began to write her name over and over. "I think you have something to say to me," Matilda said firmly, without looking up.

Ten minutes passed. She did not look at him or speak. Finally, Hannu said, "I was wrong in not obeying you."

Matilda could hear her own heart beating. "All right. You may go now."

After Hannu left and Matilda's hands stopped trembling, she went out to the field. She approached an ex-convict named Landquist. "Tomorrow you will roll the oat field."

"That's hard work," he whined, "pushing that heavy roller under a hot sun, urging that stupid horse to move. Who is going to help me?"

"One man can easily do it alone," Matilda said.

"Gentry don't know what hard work is," he retorted.

"All right. You will be given some other work to do. I will roll the oat field myself."

The next morning, at five o'clock, Matilda hitched a horse to the roller and trudged behind him. Sweat quickly soaked her eyebrows, and blisters formed on her palms. After two hours, Landquist appeared. "I apologize, Miss Wrede. I'll take over the work now."

"No, thank you," said Matilda. "You can find some other work."

She continued rolling without hesitation. By noon, she was exhausted. Her blisters broke open and oozed. She harnessed a fresh horse. Other men pleaded to be allowed to help, but she said, "No, thank you just the same." She worked until the sun set and every bone and joint flared like fire. But she finished rolling the oat field.

She hobbled to the farmhouse, sank into bed, and fell asleep instantly.

Matilda never had a problem with discipline after that day. She often heard the men brag to newcomers how "our Matilda rolled the oat field all by herself."

12

THE WORST MAN
IN FINLAND

After months of working at Toivola, Matilda began to miss visiting the prisons. She turned the operation of the farm over to Hendrik and began to travel again. A normal day of prison visiting usually began at 7:30 in the morning and ended around 6:30 at night.

Matilda's heart thrilled to see her convict friends again. But while visiting one prison, she discovered that twenty of her friends from Kakola Prison had been sent into exile in Siberia. "I must have news of them," she said to the prison governor.

"There is one man who may know something," replied the governor, a genial but worried man. "He, too, was exiled to

Siberia, but returned to Finland last week under sentence of death."

"Who is he? Where is he now? When can I see him?"

The governor shook his head. "His name is Matti Haapoja. He is in the Katajanokka Prison in Helsinki. But you cannot go into his cell. He is a murderer many times over, dangerous and violent."

"I am not afraid, for my safety is from the Lord," Matilda replied.

A week later, Matilda arrived at Katajanokka Prison, where she showed her papers of permission to the governor.

"You may visit anyone else, Miss Wrede, but I cannot allow you to go into Haapoja's cell," he said. "My job is at stake, perhaps my freedom and life, if any harm comes to you."

After much discussion, Matilda was allowed to go as far as Haapoja's cell door. There, two wardens also gave warnings. "Please, Miss Wrede, do not even consider going in. This prisoner has been in a ferocious mood since he returned from Siberia. He committed many crimes there."

"That makes it even more important that someone point him to God. Do not worry. The Lord bears the responsibility for my safety, not you."

A guard unlocked the heavy wooden door and Matilda stepped into the cell, catching her breath because of the rancid smell. On the wooden pallet hinged to the wall lay an enormous man with a gray prison blanket pulled over his head. She cleared her throat and waited. No sound. No movement. "Matti Haapoja?" She stepped closer and touched his shoulder. "Are you sleeping?"

The giant of a man leaped out of his bed, lifting the heavy chains as if they were feathers. "Who are you?" the prisoner shouted in a deep, rumbling voice. "Who dares disturb the sleep of Matti Haapoja?" His bushy mustache almost covered the lower part of his handsome, otherwise clean-shaven face.

"My name is Matilda," she said. "I am—"

Before she could finish, the huge man threw his chains across her neck, slammed her body against the wall, and tightened the chain. Matilda felt herself on the verge of fainting, but she looked steadily into his eyes and whispered, "God will not allow this."

He cocked his head and stared at her, then backed away, lowering the chains.

"I have friends who were sent into exile in Siberia," she said, rubbing her tender neck. She mentioned their names. "I was hoping you could give me news of them."

Matti laughed, the eerie sound filling the cell. "I know who you are. You are Governor Wrede's daughter. He is one of the most good-looking men I have ever laid eyes on. You are almost as tall, and you have his nose."

Matilda smiled. "We can't all be as handsome as Pappa, or as Matti Haapoja."

Matti sat on the pallet, a grin tugging at his lips.

"Aren't you going to invite me to sit?" she asked.

His expression told Matilda that she had taken him off guard, but he edged over. "And would you dare to sit beside Matti Haapoja?" Matilda joined him on the pallet and he flashed a dazzling smile. "Now, don't you go talking religion to me. I'm the worst man in Finland. My sins are as high as a mountain."

"Thank God they are," she said. "A mountain has many little cracks and crevices where seeds may be sown. Someday we will talk about it. But for now, tell me about life in Siberia."

"I worked in the mines," he said. "I also did some construction work and hauled logs when the temperature was forty degrees below zero. You here in Finland don't know what cold is. Imagine a weasel hanging on to your fingertips, gnawing at them. The cold doesn't completely numb a person, but it's always there. There's no relief from the gnawing weasel."

He spoke as one who had been educated, or at least read books. "My eyes froze shut. My frozen sweat encased me like a mummy's wrappings. I longed for death every day."

He shivered as he stared at the wall behind her. "This place isn't much better. But I may be transferred soon. To Tavastehus."

"The women's prison?" Matilda asked.

"Yes. Some of my crimes were committed in that district, so the trial must be reopened there. My sister is a warden at Tavastehus."

"Tarja?" Yes, now she saw the resemblance.

"Do you know her?"

"I met her once," Matilda said. "She is a capable woman with strong convictions."

"She took my life of crime very hard. She had noble plans for me and worked to provide money for my schooling. She's an upright and moral soul, but a bit of a Pharisee. I'm not sure what kind of greeting I'll get from her. We grew up close, but then everything changed."

The warden announced it was time for Matilda to leave Matti's cell. Matilda said good-bye and went on to visit others. She visited fourteen prisoners that day. With some she stayed for hours, others only a few minutes, depending upon the state of mind of the prisoner. A few acted cruel, but most were friendly. One lied with every word he uttered.

That evening, the prison governor offered Matilda a small guest room at his home. "You are welcome to stay here whenever you are in the area," the governor's wife said.

Like Elijah's room, Matilda thought, *though I'm far from being a prophet.*

"The greatest need of the prisoners," she told the governor as they sat by the fireplace sipping tea, "is someone to talk to. Not to talk to them, but someone who will listen."

"Our work is to see the prisoners humbled and broken," the governor told her. "It is not fitting for you to bring new life and hope to such depraved men."

"A prisoner does not need to be told he is worthless and wicked," Matilda answered. "He already feels great guilt. I look for something good in each one, no matter how small. That makes a beginning for him to open his heart and soul to the love of God. We must love those whom we seek to save without waiting until we find something lovable in them."

Matilda looked into the governor's confused eyes.

"One of my favorite Scriptures is Isaiah 38:17. The Lord has loved my soul out of the pit of corruption. If God wins people in this way, why should I not imitate Him?"

She returned to the prison at 6:30 the following morning and again visited until 7:30. As she walked to the governor's house, exhausted and discouraged, she passed by a grassy slope at the edge of town. The day was still hot. The cobblestones, which had been collecting heat all day, seemed to throw it up at her.

Two men in rags were lounging on the grass quarreling over a brown bottle, trying to pull out the cork. Matilda recognized them as ex-convicts, both of whom had professed Christ in prison. Too worn out to speak, she glanced at them and kept going.

"Did you see her sad eyes?" she overheard one say to the other.

"She does not approve of what we're doing."

The first man stood with a shout. Matilda swung around. "To the health of Matilda Wrede!" He up-ended the bottle and poured the yellow, foaming beer out into the grass.

Matilda ran over to him. "Did you do that for my sake?" she asked breathlessly. He nodded. "You must have been looking forward to your drink on this dreadfully hot day, yet you poured it out. Tell me true, did you do it for me?"

"Yes," the man assured her.

"Sit down a minute." Matilda sank onto the cool grass and took off her bonnet. "Today has been so discouraging. I longed for a little cheer, just a speck of encouragement.

And you have given it to me, better than I could have wished. This is probably the loveliest thing you have done in your entire lives. You went without a pleasure to give me pleasure. Now, you must both come with me to the little coffee shop in town and we'll have an iced drink and some cinnamon buns."

She stood, but the men held back. "We're not dressed proper," one said. "You are a fine lady. You don't want to be seen with men like us."

"You are fit company for anyone," she told them happily. "Men who could make a sacrifice like you did are true gentlemen."

She placed her right hand on one man's arm and her left on the other's, and they strolled together to the coffee house.

13

IN PRISON
FOR CHRISTMAS

On Christmas Eve at Rabbelugn, Matilda knew, Pappa and Helena and the married brothers and sisters and their little ones would all be making merry. They would sit in the dining room around the fifteen-foot-high fireplace. And all the visiting aunts and uncles would ask in surprise, "Where's Matilda?"

Helena and the cook would have worked for weeks baking ginger cookies, prune tarts, and braided cardamom bread. Matilda closed her eyes for a moment and could almost smell the bread hot from the oven. Rabbelugn would be a regular music box of a house, full of laughter and children and pets.

But in Kakola Prison, the halls were cold

and dreary. Matilda stood in the corridor, shivering. The days had grown shorter and darker in December. Wet snow stuck to the sides of buildings. Umbrellas in the street blew inside out. Gray rain, cold sleet, nasty wind. The bay froze.

From a dirty window, Matilda looked down on the town and its cemetery. Hundreds of candles twinkled at the grave sites. Thousands more shone in windows.

Matilda remembered how she and Pekka had made iced candle holders. They filled dozens of buckets with water. In two or three hours the water froze, beginning at the edges, leaving a small hollow in the center. They dumped the buckets upside down so the water in the center could run out. Then they turned the icy holders onto the ground and lit candles in the cavities.

Matilda remembered the year Pekka was a Starboy. He and two other boys went from house to house dressed as young wise men, singing about the Christ Child. They wore white robes and carried wands with gold stars. Wherever they sang, they were given Christmas treats.

Christmas Day would find most families in early-morning church. But tonight, families were enjoying the Christmas Eve dinner. Appetizers of fish and roe drenched in sauce. Cold cuts and salads. Baked ham with prunes and a rutabaga casserole. Raisin cakes, nuts, and fruit would top off the meal.

But Matilda had no desire to eat. There was no Christmas spirit at Kakola. The corridor was silent except for the clanking of chains and the moans of prisoners. She clutched the copies of the Christmas letter she'd written for them and wondered if it would make the holiday a bit less unbearable for some.

Selma, the prison cook, pattered down the hall carrying a mug of hot cocoa. "Dear Miss Wrede, won't you take this to ward off the chill?"

Matilda gratefully took the cocoa.

"And please come taste the Christmas loaves before they go into the oven," Selma requested. "The baker would not dream of making them without your approval."

Matilda followed her to the kitchen. She tasted a few pinches of dough. Christmas loaves were the only things the prisoners were given to eat that had a little sugar in them. She pronounced them delicious.

"Would you scrape the leftover pieces of dough from around the kettle and make me a small loaf?" Matilda asked. "I would be so happy to have a Christmas gift."

The baker, with as much flour in his brown hair as on his hands, replied, "Oh, no, not from scraps. The first loaf, the biggest loaf, will be for you."

Selma stepped closer to Matilda and said softly, "I put a whole egg and extra sugar in your loaf. I will bring it to you when it is baked."

Matilda smiled at the two, then returned to the corridor. In the silence, she heard whispered messages being passed from cell to cell. "Matilda Wrede is here tonight. It would not do for her to hear us complain or groan on Christmas Eve. We must try not to, for her sake." She visited every cell, distributing her Christmas letter.

Just before midnight, the silence was broken by the sound of screaming and cursing. Two guards and two wardens rushed to the cell of a man named Topi. Matilda followed.

Topi paced his cell like a wild animal, flashing a shoemaker's knife. "I have sworn by a solemn oath to take a life before midnight tonight. I'll either kill a guard or I'll kill myself. And you know I am a man of my word."

"Fetch me a mattress," called the warden. "We'll all go into the cell and smash him against the wall. Once we get him in irons, he can go to the underground dungeon for the holidays."

"No," cried Matilda. "You can't do such a cruel thing on Christmas Eve, when we celebrate the birthday of the King of love. Topi must be won by love."

The wardens and guards stared at her.

"Let me go in," she said.

Topi's cell door was unlocked. Matilda walked up to him and said, "Topi, give me the knife."

"Never." He glared at her with glassy eyes.

Ignoring her fear, Matilda continued in a soft, soothing voice. "On Christmas, many years ago, divine love came down from heaven to earth. There will be no life taken today."

"But I made a vow to kill myself or someone else. You've said yourself that we should always keep our promises."

"I am glad to hear you are a man of your word. Perhaps you could give me the knife as a Christmas present."

He shook his head stubbornly.

Matilda sent up a quick prayer for her safety and for Topi's temper. "All right," she said playfully, "then I must take it away from you."

He snorted. "Go ahead and try," he said, holding out his powerful clenched hand. As if playing a game with a child, she unbent his fingers one by one. In moments the knife was hers. She dropped it into her pocket.

She sat and talked to Topi for two hours, until the rage passed. Then she turned to the warden, who shook his head and escorted her back up the corridor. "Please don't report Topi," she said. "Not on Christmas Eve." She handed over the knife.

The warden smiled. "I'll be happy to do that for you, Miss Wrede."

As they neared the exit, Selma came running toward Matilda with the Christmas loaf. Matilda thanked them both, then headed for the governor's residence and her little room there. The town twinkled with candles. All over the world, she knew, Christians were singing "Joy to the World." But there was no joy in the prison.

Lord, Matilda prayed as she approached her temporary home, *come into the lonely cells of the prisoners and give them hope, love, and salvation. And please call other Christians who will take up the burden of Your work. For who will visit these men when I am gone?*

She rang the bell at the front door and was quickly ushered in by the governor's maid, Meimi. "Let me make you some hot tea," she said, and Matilda followed her to the kitchen. "I fixed up your bed," said Meimi, who was small and shy. "I put the warming pan under the covers with hot coals in it."

"Warm toes for Christmas Eve." Matilda smiled at her, gratefully accepting the cup of tea. "Thank you, Meimi."

She began slicing her Christmas loaf. "Would you like a piece?"

"Oh, no, thank you just the same," Meimi said. She shivered and looked over her shoulder. "I'd be afraid to eat anything from the prison."

Matilda didn't insist. "Good night, then," she said. "And thank you. Warm toes are a lovely Christmas present."

But Matilda lay awake all night thinking of the prisoners who could not sleep because their feet ached from the cold.

14

THE BONE
IN THE SOUP

The following week Matilda traveled to Helsinki, where she stayed with a friend, Captain Hedwig von Haartman, a tall, ruddy-cheeked woman who worked with the Salvation Army. Matilda arrived quite late and went straight to her bed. In the morning she awoke to the smell of fresh-baked bread. From the distinct aroma, Matilda knew Hedwig was baking *rieska,* a flat bread made of potato and barley flours. She heard the scrape of the long wooden spatula as her friend pulled the loaf out of the oven.

From her narrow window, Matilda saw a typical Finnish early morning, black as the inside of a cooking kettle. Wind tromboned down the narrow street. Hail rattled against the glass like steel springs.

"Come on, legs, bend," Matilda coaxed. So many hours standing on cold, damp prison floors had made her joints stiff and tender. She slipped into her black dress and fastened the silver brooch at her neck.

"Good morning, Baroness," Hedwig greeted her as she descended the stairs.

"Don't 'Baroness' me, Captain," Matilda retorted with a wide smile. "You know I am simply the prisoner's friend, as everyone calls me." Matilda sipped hot coffee and bit hungrily into the *rieska*. "I must speak to Viktor today."

"Isn't he the convict who tried to steal your brooch when you visited the prison last?"

"He never intended to steal it. He only asked to hold it in his hands for an hour. Then he returned it, looking quite pleased with himself. I can't imagine why. He's a life-termer and will die in prison. He's heard the Gospel many times, and I long to know if he has accepted Christ as Savior. He was so quiet the last time I saw him."

"Sullen?"

"Not sullen. Depressed. Or perhaps making escape plans. Who knows a prisoner's heart? Only the Lord who loves him."

Hedwig offered Matilda a small dish. "Would you like a bit of marmalade?"

Matilda's hand twitched to accept it, but she shook her head. "I recently decided I will eat only prisoner's fare. And the prisoners know it."

"Have some rice pudding then," Hedwig insisted. "You must keep up your strength."

Matilda knew a sensible argument when she heard one. She savored a few spoonfuls of the scrumptious treat.

"Wrap up tight," said Hedwig as Matilda prepared to leave. "Take the extra scarf. And hurry back for supper. I'm making pea soup."

As she braced against the wind, Matilda reveled in the delightful prospect of pea soup at day's end. But she wondered how her stomach would respond. Lately, she had pains that came and went at the oddest times. She felt weak, but she didn't dare miss a day of visiting the prisoners. They all looked forward to seeing her. Nobody else loved them the way she did. No one thought they could be reformed, or even deserved to be. Matilda always spoke quietly and with patience, not preaching but talking of God's great love for them.

"Good morning," she greeted the warden, who scowled at her. Like everyone else, he did not approve of a baroness visiting men who lived like animals. He grumbled as he led her to the cells.

Viktor sat on the cold, damp floor. His long, thin face folded into itself, creased from loss of body fat, but he was smiling. In his filthy outstretched hand Matilda saw a delicate ivory brooch.

She took it and cradled it in her palm. It was the exact image of her silver brooch, but much lovelier. The words *Armo ja Rauha* were carved in the center. "Did you make this?"

"For you, Miss Wrede," he said, his eyes shining.

"Where did you get ivory?"

"Seven months ago I had a truly awful bowl of cabbage soup for supper. Not a bit of meat, not even a vegetable peeling. Just greasy water with a big piece of bone. I saved the bone, and washed it every day, and dried it in the sun for weeks. Then I worked for seven months carving with a little nail I found."

"That's why you borrowed my silver pin for an hour," Matilda said.

"Yes, to fix the design in my mind. I wanted to give you a gift for your sacrifice in coming here to visit us."

Matilda's eyes teared. "It's lovely," she said. Removing the silver pin at her throat, she dropped it into her dress pocket. She fastened the pin of bone at her neck. "I will always wear it."

"That is not all." Viktor hunched forward. "Just as I have made something beautiful out of a soup bone, God made me, Viktor, as bad as any man ever born, into something good. Remember how many times you told me the Lord of love could save a man like me and turn him into something fine? Well, God has cleaned up my sins, just like the sun bleached that bone white."

He lowered his head. "Soon I will die for my crimes. I die a sinner, but a pardoned one. I'm just a bone in the soup, but I am also a jewel for His crown."

Matilda was speechless. She listened to Viktor talk about the Lord while hours passed. She knew the streets would be dark and deserted and Hedwig would be heating up the pea soup. But she couldn't tear herself away.

Finally she stood and bade Viktor good night. As she walked down the hall, she heard cries from all the cells.

"Miss Wrede! We have waited all day to see you. I have not talked to you for weeks. Don't go yet. Please don't leave."

Matilda stopped. "I will stay awhile longer. You may come to me one at a time in the vacant cell where the warden has given me a little table and two chairs. Be sure to thank the warden for his kindness in allowing you out of your cell."

By the time the final prisoner concluded his visit, Matilda was faint from hunger. She hurried down the corridor, eager to get home and taste that pea soup. Near the exit was a room that served as the prison hospital. She stopped and looked in. Seven men lay in silent gloom, staring at the dirty ceiling.

Depression wrapped around her as she stepped into the room. Seven sets of mournful eyes turned toward her. "Do you know that you can do some good in the world, even though you are flat in bed?" she asked.

The mournful eyes didn't change.

"It's true. You may feel useless, but cheerful thoughts will help you get better. And they will help the men on each side of your bed. If you have thoughts of hate and revenge, you not only harm yourselves, but you lay a burden on those around you. You might believe the prison governor is unfair, or the warden cruel, and they may be. But you are only doing harm to yourself by complaining."

A few of the men struggled to sit up and listen.

"Your thoughts can reach up to heaven and to the living God. Don't waste time on thoughts that are bitter and dark."

One prisoner, with a thin yellowed face, clawed his fingernails into his pillow. "We all had thoughts of you this morning. When the train pulled in, we heard its whistle through the open window and it seemed to say, 'Matilda Wrede is coming today! Matilda Wrede is coming today!' And here you are. We waited all day hoping you would have time for us."

Matilda couldn't speak. She had almost passed them by. "Of course I have time for you. I'll visit tomorrow and stay longer. I'll bring apples, would you like that?"

They nodded with great enthusiasm.

"In the meantime," she said, "remember that you may reach God through your thoughts if you lift up your heart in prayer in Jesus' name. You can walk in fellowship with Him and He will use you to bless your world."

She knew they didn't want her to go, but she felt on the verge of illness from lack of food and rest. She said good-bye and started the long walk back to Hedwig's house. She felt shaky and her feet stumbled. "I wonder what day it is," she murmured to herself. "Have I missed supper or breakfast or both? Did I sleep last night?" Finally she spotted Hedwig's porch light. "I do hope she saved a drop of soup and a bite of crust. Such a feast that would be."

15

FORSBERG, THE BURGLAR

Before Matilda left Helsinki, she held a service in the dormitory for the prisoners who were allowed out of their cells. She spoke to them of God's love and His desire to save everyone.

After her talk, one man stayed behind. He had big brown eyes and a boyish face full of longing. "Pardon me, Miss," he said. "My name is Forsberg. I'm a burglar."

"I am pleased to meet you, Forsberg," Matilda said.

"May I ask you a question?"

"Of course."

"God's love is not for me, is it?" he asked wistfully.

"No one is beyond the reach of God's love," said Matilda. "Reach out to Him. He's reaching for you."

"I can't." Forsberg hung his head. "I'm too bad. I've been in and out of every prison in Finland. I'm getting shipped off to the mines in Siberia the day after tomorrow."

Matilda was appalled. Exile was the worst fate for a prisoner. Forsberg would probably never see family, home, or his beloved country again. "I must leave here tomorrow," she said.

He looked up at her with a confused, haunted expression.

"I promised to visit Abo Prison, which is not far from here. But I will come back to say good-bye."

Another prisoner came up to them. "I am being sent to Siberia as well," he said. "My name is Jari." He reached into his pocket and pulled out a wedding ring. "They will take this away from me," he said. "Please, Miss, Wrede, if you can, would you give this ring to my wife in Lapland? Her name is Sirkka. Tell her we are united forever in love, even though I will never see her again."

Matilda took the ring. "If the Lord provides the opportunity, I will certainly do this for you, Jari," she promised.

Early the next morning, Matilda started off for Abo. Finland's oldest city, eight hundred years old, lay scattered along the Aurajoke River. It began as a trading post on the Aura River and had been the center of Swedish Finland. The city was still used for shipbuilding, and the river was alive with the history of battles, pirates, and merchants.

In the center of the city stood a castle that towered over the town, built of enormous blocks of granite. The castle had once boasted forty furnished rooms. There was an entire suite of royal rooms for the King of Sweden, should he chance to visit. A banquet hall, a shooting gallery, and a ballroom kept the servants busy. Priceless paintings, tapestries, and hand-carved furniture had filled the rooms.

In 1614, a fire gutted the castle, and it fell into ruin. Now it was used as a prison. Elderly convicts lay neglected and ailing within its massive walls.

Matilda stopped to sit on a stone ledge to rest a few minutes. She watched numerous ships sail by. Small craft stores crowded the streets—pawn shops, shoemakers, chandlers, and crafters of clocks, dolls, birdhouses, stuffed animals.

She wished she had time to explore all that was Abo, but inside the castle people needed her and the message of hope she could bring them. She rose and approached the castle entrance.

She was welcomed inside, given lunch, and allowed to hold a service. Thirty-eight prisoners, most of them feeble and frail, came to listen.

After the service, an old man hobbled up to her. "Thank you for coming," he said. "You are the first person to show me friendship from the heart. God bless you."

Another elderly man interrupted them, his pale blue eyes glazed and unfocused. "I am a Christian," he said. "But I'm almost blind. I can't read my Bible any longer. I just sit and hold it in my hands."

Matilda wrote down their names. "I am putting together a mailing list for holiday letters. I already have one thousand names, but there's always room for more."

Leaving the Abo Prison, Matilda started down the

steep, moss-covered steps of the castle. Near the bottom she tripped and fell hard, her right foot bending under her. She heard the snap of bone. Tears poured down her face. She forced herself to stand. "In the name of Jesus of Nazareth, I will walk." She motioned to a nearby droshky, the low four-wheeled Russian carriage. The driver ran toward her, his silver-buckled beaver hat wobbling. "Madame, you are hurt. Let me take you to a doctor."

As the driver helped her into the carriage, Matilda thought for a moment. Common sense told her to go directly to a doctor. Then she thought of Forsberg's troubled face and the yearning he had for God, which he did not even recognize. A doctor would insist she go home to Rabbelugn immediately.

"Take me to Kakola Prison," she instructed the driver, climbing onto the bench of the droshky.

The driver drove slowly, but the ride was still bumpy and painful. When they reached Kakola, Matilda limped to Forsberg's cell. His face shone with joy. "Miss Wrede," he cried. "You spoke true. God does love me. Jesus is mine and I am His." He covered his face with his big hands and burst into happy tears.

Oh, the pain is worth this, Matilda thought. *And I might have missed it, had I not kept my promise to come back.*

"Do you know when I decided your religion must be true?" asked Forsberg. "When I was told you went into the cells alone, without a warden or guard. You trusted us, and that made me want to hear more of your God."

Matilda sat beside Forsberg on his pallet, unable to speak.

"Miss Wrede," Forsberg said, "may I measure your foot?" At Matilda's confused expression, he explained. "Before I came here, I was a shoemaker. When I get to Siberia I would like to make you a beautiful pair of soft Russian boots with fur inside so you will never have cold feet again."

Matilda stretched out her right foot. The skin was puffed and blue, swollen over the top of her shoe.

"Miss Wrede," Forsberg exclaimed. "What happened?" She told him of her fall. "You should have gone to the doctor at once."

"First, I had to come here," she said. "Like I promised."

"You did this for me?" he said, almost weeping.

As Matilda limped back to the droshky, Forsberg and Jari stood in silent awe, staring at the woman who cared so much about their eternal souls.

Matilda's ankle had a complicated break and she stayed at the prison governor's house for four weeks, until it was safe to move her to Rabbelugn. The chaplain visited her every day and brought messages from her convict friends. A collection of money was taken from the prison staff and presented to her just before she left. The prison governor paid for a proper carriage so she could ride home in comfort.

Pappa carried Matilda into the house and up to her room. Helena wept. "Tilda, darling, please stay home for a while. You can write to the prisoners. I'll be your secretary and your nurse."

Their father's face looked grave. "She doesn't weigh

much," he said. "Helena, tell Cook to send up nourishing trays for this girl."

"I want to prepare every morsel with my own hands," Helena cried.

Cook stayed awake nights consulting old cookbooks handed down by her grandmother to find the most delicious recipes. Away from the daily sight of suffering prisoners, Matilda's appetite grew. "I feel like a stuffed owl," she told Helena one day.

After a few weeks, the doctor allowed Matilda to put weight on her right foot, but insisted she use a cane. She tried to follow his orders, but found the cane awkward. One morning, she dropped it down from her window and told Pekka to hide it. Holding on to the banister, she made her way down the long winding staircase to the dining room.

"I must go back to Kakola," she told Pappa and Helena at breakfast. "Many prisoners there need me."

Her father sighed. "Tilda, darling, is there no one else who can do this work? Perhaps some good person will step forward and get the laws changed."

"Pappa," Matilda cried, "the public doesn't know what's going on at the prisons. And even if someone changed the laws, that's not the same as friendship. The prisoners must know they have a friend outside the prison."

"But you are giving yourself away," protested Helena. "You were positively frail when you first came home. Soon there will be nothing left of you."

"God gives more grace the more we need it," Matilda

said. She felt a particularly strong urge to visit Matti Haapoja again. He was so in need of grace. If he could be converted, and if he could be pardoned, what a giant of a witness he would be to his people.

Matilda's heart sank as she realized she was only day-dreaming. The man was a murderer several times over. To imagine him free and witnessing was wishful thinking on a grand scale. Still, with God anything was possible.

16

MERCY AT MIDNIGHT

As Matilda made plans to visit Matti Haapoja, she received a call from her friend, Miss Ullner. "I'm taking a trip to the winter market at Rovaniemi near the Arctic Circle," she said. "I belong to the Finnish SPCA and they asked me to report on the condition of the reindeer herds in Lapland." She invited Matilda to accompany her.

Lapland! Matilda had been praying for a way to deliver Jari's wedding ring to his wife. She accepted Miss Ullner's invitation at once. Amazed at God's providential arrangements, Matilda found the wedding ring and tied it in the corner of a handkerchief.

Matilda and Miss Ullner traveled north by train as far as they could, almost to the great peat lands and treeless moors. Pine was the last tree seen as they climbed above the timberline. All around were swamps, covered with snow. The long Arctic night crept over the land and seemed to Matilda to be an endless, violet-colored dusk.

Miss Ullner spoke Lappish and had made friends years ago with a family she met on a previous visit. The father, Vilho, came to meet them with a *pulkka,* a boat-shaped sledge on one runner, drawn by reindeer. He wore a "cap of the four winds" on his head. The corners of the brightly colored cap flopped down over his ears.

"This is a delightful experience," Matilda said as they rode swiftly over the snow.

"You are in the Land of the Midnight Sun," Miss Ullner told her. "Snow falls here from the middle of September to late April. When we go to the winter market in Rovaniemi, you will see Finns, Lapps, Norwegians, Russians, and Swedes."

Matilda laughed. "I came prepared," she said, showing her friend a basket full of Gospel leaflets in all four languages. "I shall sling this over my arm and get acquainted with the people."

Vilho stopped in front of a beautiful log cabin. Before Matilda was even in the doorway, a mug of hot coffee was placed into her hands by Vilho's wife.

"Don't tell me," Matilda said, noting the size and shape of all the fur boots lined up on the porch. "You have five children."

"Six," corrected Miss Ullner. "A four-year-old boy, a seven-year-old girl, two ten year olds, a teenager, and a baby. The newborn doesn't walk yet, but he wears tiny boots of reindeer skin. He has his own little sled where he's strapped in for safety, wrapped in furs."

The adults gathered around a large black cookstove. Vilho's father played folk songs on his *kantele*, a flat stringed instrument he held on his lap. Strange woodland sounds poured out of the *kantele* and the grandfather sang the lyrics under his breath. Vilho joined him on a violin, and music rained down from his fingertips.

After playing several songs, the old man leaned back in his chair. "I have the Old Faith," he said. "I believe in the spirits of the woods and the waterfalls, the spirits of clouds and air. Do you?" He looked at Matilda earnestly, his bushy white hair falling to his shoulders. White eyebrows fuzzed his face.

"I have known the spirit of silence and peace in the woods," Matilda answered. "I have waded in the water and felt the spirit of purity and coolness. There is a spirit of beauty when one looks over Lake Tanajarvi's crystal waters. But over them all is the Father God in heaven, the God of love."

For the next several days, Matilda spoke to Vilho's father of the Lord Jesus and God's salvation. He listened intently and finally realized that the craving of his heart was not for nature, but for nature's Creator. He accepted Christ as his Savior and was born again. "I am a very old man," he said, "so old I don't even remember my age. But God has shown mercy to me at the midnight of my life."

"Mercy at midnight," Matilda repeated. "That's how it has been in the prisons too. Many men have been converted to Christ at the last moment, just before their execution.

Mercy at midnight. I thank you for making me see it that way."

Finally, the weather cleared enough for Matilda and Miss Ullner to attend the winter market. "Tell me more of the reindeer," Matilda said as they took the sledge into town.

Miss Ullner leaned back against the side of the sled as they flew smoothly atop the snow. "These huge, beautiful animals supply almost everything the Lapps need. Meat and milk. Clothes and shoes and boots. The bones and antlers are carved into tools and needles. Their sinews are dried and used as thread. The Finnish government has sent me to report on the slaughter of large herds. There have been rumors there is some cruelty involved."

The winter market was held on a large piece of acreage belonging to the Lapps. Thousands of reindeer were herded together near a corral, waiting to be branded, sold, traded, or slaughtered. On the frozen lake, several Lapps were ski-racing behind reindeer. Matilda wandered over to watch the lasso-throwing contest.

Miss Ullner grasped Matilda's arm and led her to a quieter section of the market. "The women here sell crafts and baked goods, woven rugs and shirts. Aren't their costumes beautiful? All the colors of fall."

Matilda admired the russet, orange, red, and gold outfits for a moment, then stopped suddenly when she heard her name being sung somewhere. She looked around. "Listen," she said. "Someone calls me."

Miss Ullner lifted her earflaps. "Someone is singing

about you," she exclaimed. "Over there. That small man on the wooden platform."

They hurried to the area where the man continued to sing in a pleasing baritone.

> Matilda Wrede! Oh, she of compassion
> Looked on our need and helped us so.
> Matilda Wrede, the prisoner's friend,
> Drank of our sorrow and cup of woe.

"Why, it's Reino," Matilda cried. "He was in Kakola Prison."

The man sang fourteen more verses. When he finished, Matilda rushed toward him. "Reino! How is it with you?"

The singer stood and grasped her hands with joy. "This is she," he cried to the crowd. "Here is the one I sing about. Gather around, friends. This is Matilda Wrede in the flesh. Preach to them, Miss Wrede."

Matilda studied the men and women pushing closer to see her. "I don't speak Lappish," she whispered to Reino. "Will you translate?"

"Of course."

"Dear friends," Matilda said, with Reino repeating her words in Lappish. "I want to tell you about my best friend, Jesus." She explained the Gospel and told of God's wonderful love. Then she moved through the crowd, placing tracts in every hand. The Lapps were pleased to find leaflets in their own language.

That evening, back at the cabin, Matilda asked Vilho,

"Do you know of a married Lapp woman named Sirkka whose husband, Jari, is being sent to Siberia?"

"Oh, yes, we know Sirkka, poor girl."

"I have a personal message for her," Matilda said.

"We can take the sledge to her cabin after supper," Vilho said. "It isn't far."

That night, Matilda bundled up and stepped outside. The dark sky was streaked with scarlet waves of light that made the snow look stained with blood. The luminescent ribbons slid sideways, then retreated, then turned to silver and yellow spears that fell from the heavens. Ripples of light seemed to seep from space and drip through cracks in the night sky.

"What is it?" she cried out in alarm. "What's happening?"

"The northern lights," Miss Ullner explained. "The aurora borealis. Have you never seen it?"

"No." Matilda stood breathless. "It looks almost like the Second Coming, so sudden, so beautiful and spiritual."

They watched for a quarter hour until the northern lights faded away. Then they set off for Sirkka's cabin.

Jari's wife was a tall girl with a long brown braid and a face full of devotion. She eagerly led Matilda and Miss Ullner to a carved rocking chair that seated three people. As they rocked before the wood stove, Sirkka took Matilda's hand. "Miss Wrede, you are an important person high up in the church, are you not?"

"Not at all. My work of visitation is mine alone."

"Can you marry people?"

Matilda was puzzled. "Why do you ask?"

"Jari and I were wed in the church years ago. But I would like to repeat my vows, to make them sure. It isn't likely that Jari will be tempted by women in Siberia. Oh, no, the temptations will all be mine. Men have already come around, offering to court me." She rocked faster and her pretty face was full of grief. "It isn't easy for a girl alone to survive here. My two small children and I shall have to go back to my parents' cabin, although they can scarcely afford three more mouths to feed. It is sorely tempting for me to stray, but I do not wish to. Please, Miss Wrede, would you marry us again? I know it will keep me true to him."

Matilda couldn't speak for the pain in her throat. Finally, she said, "If it will help you, Miss Ullner and I will hear you renew your vows. But you were already joined by God, and no one can improve upon that."

Matilda reached into her pocket and pulled out Jari's ring. Sirkka gasped.

"Wear this on your right hand, where you will always see it."

Matilda and Miss Ullner gazed into the gem-colored fire as Sirkka renewed her vows to God for a husband she would never see again.

17

LET THERE
BE LIGHT!

After Matilda's trip to Lapland, she spent the rest of the year at home in Rabbelugn with her father and Helena. Helena delighted in spoiling her and letting her sleep late. She stuffed her with nourishing stews and creamy desserts. But Matilda felt strangely out of place. It seemed almost a sin to live like this, surrounded by so much luxury.

One morning, as Matilda sat in a balcony window with her father and sister, Helena asked, "How is your ankle, Tilda?"

"I'm worried about that too," Father added. "I notice you limp and bite back the pain when you put weight on it. I'm convinced it didn't heal properly."

Matilda tried to laugh them off. "It's my thorn in the flesh," she said, "given to keep me humble. Should I be more favored than the apostle Paul?"

"Tell us the truth," Father said. "How do you feel?"

"Mornings are the worst," she conceded. "My ankle is stiff and the pain shoots all the way up to my shoulder. Getting out of bed is like crawling out of the grave."

Helena dropped her knitting and shuddered. "And still you keep going to the prisons for long hours each day?"

Matilda glanced at her father. There was much more white in his hair now, on both sides and over his forehead. *That is my doing,* she thought. But the more she studied the Bible, the more she saw that suffering was part of a Christian's life. The ones who loved her most suffered too.

A realization hit Matilda like a flash of lightning. Father hadn't *retired* from his governorship—he had *resigned.* Hoping to save her from the difficult life she had chosen, he sacrificed his career and the beloved home in Vasa, his friends and social life, to move her away from the prisoners. Suddenly she understood the extent of his love for her.

With a heavy heart, she sat on the edge of his chair and put an arm around his shoulder. "Pappa, I did not choose this work. God called me. I could not say no to Him."

Pappa shook his head. "Tilda, my daughter, I no longer have any objections. I can see God is blessing your ministry."

Matilda paced, trying not to limp. "I must continue fighting the prison system that locks a man in a dungeon without light or heat, chaining him by the neck until he dies or goes mad. But I wish I could find someone who would share this burden, someone who can continue visitation after I am gone."

"Tilda," her father said quietly, "this helper you hope for must also be called by God. Do not err in this. Wait for the Lord to send a helper, if it be His will."

Matilda sat in the window seat to rest her ankle. "Of course," she said quietly.

A few days later, Matilda took the train to Katajanokka Prison in Helsinki, where Matti was still held. She carried her Bible, though she had determined she would not speak to him of God unless he spoke first. Anything else would only harden his heart.

The warden unlocked Matti's cell door and she stepped in. The heavy wooden door closed behind her with a thud.

"Well, Haapoja, how is it with you?"

He stood, so tall he seemed to fill up all the space in the cell. A look of astonishment crossed his face. "You came back," he exclaimed. "Why?"

"I promised," she said. "We are friends, and I always keep a promise to a friend."

He scowled and began to pace, swinging his muscled arms and tossing his head. "I didn't think a soul on earth cared about me," he snarled. "Then you walk in and show kindness and tell me God loves me." He rattled his chains and shouted curses at the prison system. "If God has forgiven me," he growled, "why can't men also forgive? Why chain me up like a mad dog?"

Matilda placed her hand on his muscular arm. "Won't

you sit down with me?" She motioned to the pallet. "I'd like to rest my feet."

"Prisoners must stand when anyone comes in the cell. That is the rule."

"No one is around, and I'm asking you." She sat, resting her Bible in her lap.

He sat beside her and pointed to a crack in the wooden door. "See that big dent? One day I was allowed to use carpenter's tools in my cell. When the warden came in, I threw the ax at him. It missed and cracked the door. Now do you see the kind of man I am?"

"I see," said Matilda pleasantly.

He glared at her. "Aren't you afraid I could wring your neck? It would be easy enough."

"I'm not in the least afraid. God, my Father, watches over me. Besides, I don't think you really want to hurt me."

Matti studied her face. "Do you believe that every verse in the Bible is for our good?"

"Most assuredly. Why do you ask?"

"While we have been talking, your Bible has fallen open to the same page three times. Read from that page and see if there is any message for me."

Matilda looked down at her Bible. "Why, it's chapter one of Genesis." She read the first three verses. "Let there be light," she cried joyfully. "Oh, Matti, look into your heart. If you are honest you will admit there is darkness and confusion there. But if you believe, God will say, 'Let there be light,' and you will have a new birth."

Silence filled the cell as Matti, head in his hands, sat in deep thought. Suddenly, he threw himself on the floor and writhed in his chains. He groaned in anguish and tore his hair. Matilda joined him, calling upon God for help. The warden, frightened for her safety, opened the door a crack, but Matilda waved him away.

Finally, Matti grew still, rose, and sat with her on the pallet. His eyes were clear. "I opened my heart to God, like you said. I asked Him to shine His light in me. Now I will wait to see what He does for me. Miss Wrede, I have a big favor to ask of you. Don't go yet. The warden has probably called the chaplain and the governor and the inspectors. I don't want to see them. Please stay with me until the prison doors close for the night."

Matilda nodded. She sat with Matti until six o'clock that evening, praying and reading the Bible. She ached from head to foot, and her ankle felt on fire. But "the worst man in Finland" had surrendered to God. If somehow she could obtain a pardon for him, perhaps this could be the answer to her prayer for a helper. She pictured Matti Haapoja, over six feet tall, handsome and intelligent, speaking to convicts who would eagerly hear him.

Lord, she prayed, *bring this to pass. Use Matti for your glory.*

Before she left, she begged him to ask the warden to give him a Bible.

"I cannot." He laughed ruefully. "I used to have a pile of books, but one day I threw them in the warden's face. How I hated that man."

"Do you hate him now?"

Matti considered it. "No. No, I don't. The hatred is gone."

Matilda faltered a moment, then thrust her Bible into his hands—her Bible, with its notes and underlines that meant so much to her. "Will you accept this and read it?"

"Oh, yes, I will. I shall never throw this away. Miss Wrede, you will come again to visit, won't you?"

"I promise."

As she walked back to her lodgings, she hardly minded the pain in her ankle. The light of God had shone into Matti Haapoja's soul. What would happen now?

18

THE KING
OF HARMA
WILL GET YOU!

Matilda sat at the desk of her rented room in Helsinki staring at a letter she'd just received. It was an invitation from the King of Harma! Isotalon Antii wasn't a real king, but he owned a farm in the lake district near a town called Harma. He'd been sent to prison for some terrible deeds committed at his farmhouse, including brutal murders.

Whenever Matilda's father asked for a chain gang of prisoners to work on his estate, he always had trouble with Isotalon, who constantly started fights. One day her father put Isotalon in charge of the chain gang. "Never had a bit of trouble from him after that," Pappa said. He trusted Isotalon, and Isotalon responded to that trust.

Matilda had met Isotalon in prison. That first day, he tried to frighten her by towering over her and clanking his chains. As he looked into her fearless eyes, he dropped his arms. "You have the Land-Chief's eyes," he said in awe. "Are you Matilda Wrede, his daughter?"

"I am," she replied.

After many more visits, Isotalon became a Christian. He was devoted to Matilda and promised never to return to his former wicked life.

When Matilda was a child, the servants used to frighten her into obedience whenever she was naughty or sassy by threatening, "The King of Harma will get you if you don't behave!" She shivered at the horror stories whispered by them. His farmhouse, they said, was haunted because of the evil deeds of those who had lived there. Matilda pictured him as the wicked giant right out of the fairy tales of Hans Christian Andersen.

She chuckled at the memory. Isotalon had served his sentence. And now, the King of Harma was inviting her to his farm. Spring would be a lovely time to explore the lake country, Matilda decided.

After sending a message that she would arrive by train, she packed a luggage bag and traveled to Harma. When she got off the train, she saw a crowd of former prisoners who all knew her. But they stared at her stonily, giving no indication they recognized her. Towering head and shoulders above them was Isotalon. A chill went down Matilda's spine. Had this powerful man lured her to his farmhouse in order to murder her? Perhaps he had not really changed.

She walked toward the men, struggling with her bag.

No one offered to help her. Not one man raised his cap in respect. Matilda stood on the platform, confused.

The train started up and chugged off. Too late now to turn around and go home. When it was out of sight, Isotalon bounded forward and seized her hand. All the men lifted their caps in politeness.

"Did you notice how we didn't embarrass you?" Isotalon asked. "How we pretended not to know you? We thought you might not want the gentry on the train to see that you knew ex-convicts."

"Oh, my dear friends," Matilda said, shaking hands all around. "I am proud to know you and to find out you have made good lives for yourselves. I'm so glad to see you again."

They rode by horse and cart past small lakes and islands, through a spray of waterfalls, to Isotalon's large farmhouse. It was packed with people, who tumbled out of windows and balconies to see Matilda Wrede, the prisoner's friend. Matilda listened eagerly to their life stories and the testimonies of the ones who had found Christ in prison. She answered questions and gave a brief Bible study. Around the fireside, they held a simple prayer meeting.

When it was time for bed, Matilda was shown to a small, clean room on the second floor. Little by little the house fell silent. This was the house everyone had called "haunted." Matilda tried not to think of the awful stories, but they seemed to have a power over her mind.

Then she heard something. Furtive tiptoeing. Definitely footsteps, but soft and stealthy.

Thump! Something—someone—was trying to kick

open the door. Matilda's heart pounded. Her throat was too dry to call for help. She prayed and hung on to her pillow. She lay awake for hours, listening to the silence. Finally, she fell asleep from exhaustion.

In the morning, Isotalon greeted her. "Did you sleep well, Miss Wrede?"

"I heard noises like someone trying to break into my room."

"Oh, that was me. I felt responsible for your safety. We have so many visitors staying here this week, I decided to sleep all night outside your door. No one could bother you unless they killed me first."

After breakfast Isotalon led Matilda around the twenty-acre farm to admire the calves and piglets. "I built the barn myself," he said. "This farm is the family bank. I can borrow money on it. And I can loan out cash to my son to help him begin his own business."

After a week's pleasant visit, Matilda surprised Isotalon. "If you don't mind," she said, "I shall leave you now and explore deeper into the lake country. I have addresses for other released prisoners who wish to see me."

"How will you travel?" he asked. "Surely not on foot."

"Oh, no," Matilda assured him. "I saw a sign in town advertising a cart and horse for hire."

"Will you be going alone, Miss Wrede?" he asked.

"I'm never alone. My heavenly Father is always with me. Thank you for your hospitality, Isotalon. I have enjoyed my visit very much."

Matilda began her journey through the vast inland waterway of lakes connected by canals. Some roads ended at docks where, for a small fee, a ferry boat transported her and her cart to the next island.

What a land of beauty, she mused as she drove past yellow birch trees, berry patches, and clear waterfalls plunging deep into black pools. *Prison cells must seem especially horrible to those raised in the lake country.*

One day she stopped at an ancient well, where two old women were pulling on a rope to bring up a rusty pail. They looked as frail as dried locusts.

"That work is too hard for you, grannies," she said. "But since you have a large pailful there, may I have a small sip for my thirst?"

One elderly woman eagerly filled a dipper, and in her haste spilled the water on Matilda's dress. Frightened, she apologized over and over. "Would you like to stop and rest at the place where we live? It is called The Poorhouse. There are many of us there."

"Not this time, dears. But thank you for the cool water. It was delicious. I will pass this way again soon, on my way home, and I'll arrange a coffee party for all of you."

"That would be lovely."

The second woman stared at the brooch on Matilda's collar. "You must be rich, Miss," she said, her wispy hair hanging in her eyes. "We haven't tasted coffee since our old minister died two years ago."

"My father gave me a generous gift of money," Matilda explained. "I use it to help all those I can."

Matilda slept under the stars in the back of the cart covered with a mosquito net. The heat wrapped around her like an blanket. As she traveled, her horse helped himself to meals on the side of the road. Matilda always managed to arrive at a cottage or farmhouse just in time for supper.

A delightful existence, she thought. *But I must not forget those in chains.* She missed them and looked forward to returning.

Most of the ex-convicts lived off the beaten track, but their written directions enabled her to find them. She had some trouble locating a man named Urpo. She stopped at a farmhouse to ask help from a young man greasing the cartwheels of his farm wagon. When he looked up, she recognized him as Urpo himself.

"Miss Wrede! Is it really you?" He dropped his work, raced to the cart, lifted her out, and carried her into the house.

"Aura! Aura! Come and look. At last I can show you Miss Wrede, the one who helped me so much in prison."

Matilda stayed there two days, then started off to find Mauno, a Gypsy who had been in prison at Kakola. She stayed overnight at an inn and awoke to hear jingling bells. She saw a large cart approach with Mauno driving and the bells on the horse jangling a tune. "So it is you," he said. "I heard that a 'foreign lady' had arrived."

Matilda rode with Mauno to his farmhouse, which was the headquarters for all the Gypsies in that area. Inside, it seemed to Matilda that a box of multicolored confetti had been emptied into all the rooms. Gypsies in mismatched clothing were everywhere. The women wore lace aprons, frilly blouses, and six petticoats under their embroidered skirts. The men had knives stuck into their boot tops.

Supper that evening was vegetarian, according to Matilda's simple tastes, which Mauno remembered. Hundreds of men, women, children, and babies swarmed around outside. An old grandfather, the head of the tribe, sat in the big living room before the table. An open Bible was laid on a clean white cloth.

"He can't read," Mauno whispered, "but he knows you believe and he is showing his respect. He is the Gypsy king, as he is the oldest. There is no queen, since his wife died."

After supper, the Gypsies begged for a "Bible talk." Matilda was glad to oblige. The next evening, Mauno returned Matilda to the inn. They rode in his big cart decorated with flags, streamers, and banners. Mauno sang a lively Gypsy song. His two little boys joined in. Matilda drew curious stares from the townspeople as Mauno drove the length of the main street and pulled up at the inn with a "Whoop!"

Mauno helped her down from the cart and whispered, "I hope you won't be offended, Miss Wrede, but the old grandfather took a shine to you. He told me to ask if you would stay and wed him and become Queen of the Gypsies. He said to tell you there is a nice bit of money in it. I answered for you. I said you didn't think much of titles. Did I say the right thing?"

"Perfect." Matilda broke into helpless laughter and didn't stop even after Mauno and his boys waved good-bye from the Gypsy wagon and drove out of sight.

19

KOKKO FIRES
AND
CHURCH BOATS

Matilda traveled farther into the lake district to the farmhouse of Heikki and Laina. Heikki had served five years at Sornas Prison for counterfeiting and defrauding the government.

"I was counterfeit myself, through and through," he told everyone who would listen. "Then, because of the prison visits of Matilda Wrede, I became a new man, a new creation in Christ."

Laina was an intelligent, poetry-loving girl who had read Part I of the *Kalevala*, all 12,000 lines. The *Kalevala* was a collection of the folk tales and legends of old Finland, gathered and published by Dr. Elias Lonnrot. As in every farmhouse Matilda visited, the family owned a shelf of books called "the library." Farms and cabins were so isolated from each other that it was necessary to buy books, rather than borrow them.

Matilda unpacked her bag in the guest room of the farmhouse with its pretty handmade furniture and flowered curtains. She brushed the lint from the front of her black dress and studied her face in the mirror. Hair still mouse-brown, here and there a gray thread. Her face was thinner and paler than it had ever been. "Prison complexion," Helena had called it.

Maybe I'll go home so tanned and rosy they won't know me, Matilda thought. *This country life is so relaxing, it's positively blissful. But I dare not get used to it.*

She eyed the "Grace and Peace" pin she always wore. People everywhere were attracted to it—strangers on trains and steamers and ferries, folks in towns and cities. "It's Matilda Wrede, the one who visits prisons," they would murmur. Even here, among Christians, she wore the pin.

Matilda dined with Heikki and Laina that evening. Four little girls, aged five to ten, sat around the table. Matilda looked into their serious little faces and saw herself as a child, full of questions, wondering what life was all about. She wondered if they were being taught the wonderful Bible stories she'd always loved.

"Tomorrow is Midsummer Day," shouted Heikki while Laina piled more pancakes and berries onto Matilda's plate. "You have come at the right time. It's the greatest day of the year."

Matilda preferred Christmas and Easter, but she nodded politely. Heikki was so enthusiastic that talking to him was like walking into a burst of gunfire. At Midsummer Eve, most Finns who lived near water lit the pagan Kokko fires, huge floating bonfires to honor the ancient sun worship. In England they were called "Baal fires." Matilda never liked the idea and simply ignored the custom. The Wredes did not light Kokko fires.

After supper, the farm hands built a pile of tree trunks and branches twenty feet high on top of a hill behind the farmhouse. Barrels that once held tar were smashed up and added to the pyre.

A canal ran past Heikki's property. Matilda watched Kokko fires floating on rafts, drifting to the river. Small boats and steamers passed, so decorated with flowers and sacred birch tree bark they looked like moving islands. On a nearby lake, she saw eight Kokko fires at once.

"The fires would show up better against a dark sky," Laina said, "but Midsummer Eve is almost like daylight."

The relatives of Heikki and Laina arrived by boat or by cart, more than forty adults and handfuls of children. Heikki poured turpentine over the low branches and threw a torch into the pile of wood. Red and orange flames climbed high and were reflected in the smooth water of the canal. Everyone sang, a kind of sad chanting, but with beautiful harmony.

"Have they practiced?" Matilda asked.

Heikki shook his head. "Never. Music comes naturally to us. There are so few amusements for the lake country people, we sing all the time."

The next day, Midsummer Day, was a national holiday. The thermometer registered 95 degrees in the shade.

Matilda held Bible study talks for the relatives. A continual picnic went on outdoors.

"On Sunday," Heikki told Matilda, "we will show you something else I don't think you have ever seen. We will go to church."

"I've been to church before." Matilda laughed. "But I didn't notice a church as we traveled."

"This one isn't nearby," he replied. "Wait and see."

On Sunday, Matilda rode with Heikki and his family in a horse-drawn cart to a pier on the lake where a "church boat" waited. It looked like a giant rowboat and held as many as forty people while an additional dozen men manned the oars.

"Some families live so far from church they start out on Saturday night and carry their best clothes wrapped in a sheet. They sleep under the trees and share food with each other."

"Church must mean a great deal to them."

"Church means everything," he said simply.

Matilda enjoyed her ride across the lake, as all the people on the boat sang. The oarsmen turned the boat into small waterways where trees hung over their heads. They stopped at every island where a passenger waited.

Summer is such bud-bursting weather, Matilda thought. *We are fairly smothered with beauty.*

After an hour, she saw a sprawling pink wooden building on the far shore with at least a hundred carts and horses tethered among the trees. "Did you ever see anything like that?" Heikki asked.

Reminds me of a birthday cake, Matilda thought. "No,

indeed," she said. "I never imagined a church in this isolated area. How many people can fit in there?"

"Four thousand," Heikki said proudly. "I hope the service won't be too long for you."

"How long does it last?"

"Four hours," Laina said.

Inside, the church was warm and stuffy. Everyone wore black. The women had black silk kerchiefs on their heads. They held white handkerchiefs, and bowed their heads into them whenever they prayed. A quiet weeping swept over the congregation from time to time.

"They're weeping over their sins and their hard life," Laina whispered.

The church was jammed with people. Every so often, some left to walk outside and stretch their legs. Mothers nursed babies, and toddlers ran in and out.

Finally, the service was over and the clergyman made an announcement. "On Thursday next, I will be at home to receive your butter and eggs, potatoes and calves, for which I thank you beforehand."

Matilda was exhausted. She welcomed the picnic in the shade and the gallons of fruit juice Laina had prepared.

"What do you think of our church?" Heikki asked when they returned to his farmhouse.

Matilda pondered the question. "It was so simple and devout that I was touched. Do the people ever meet during the week?"

"No, that would be impossible. We have no clergyman to visit us."

"You are a Christian now. As head of the house you

have the right to gather family and servants together and at least read them God's Word each morning. Counting the farmhands and the cook, you could have sixteen people in your little church."

"Couldn't pray out loud," he faltered, "not in front of people."

"You need only speak a sentence of prayer," she said. "Or pray the prayers of the Bible. God will bless your family for it."

"Is this against the law?" Heikki wanted to know. "I don't want to do anything unlawful."

"God has commanded family worship," Matilda said.

"We'll do it," Laina said, her eyes shining. "I love the poetry of the Bible. Our children should be hearing the Bible stories."

"Wonderful," cried Matilda. "Now, I must be going. But do write to me. Let me know how your little church in the home is coming along."

"We will," said Heikki.

"And I will put you on my mailing list."

When she said good-bye, Matilda felt as though she was leaving a new little church behind.

Matilda hunted up the old grannies at the poorhouse, gave them gifts of coffee and money, and turned homeward. As she rode back to Harma to return the horse and cart, she mourned, *Oh, for someone to visit these scattered families.*

The thought of the simple men from this beautiful spot in Finland being chained to dungeon walls spoiled her trip and turned the sun into a grinning goblin.

She had been away from the prisons too long. Matilda could hardly wait to visit Matti Haapoja again.

20

NO MIRACLES
TODAY

Helena, worried over her sister's health, went apartment-hunting in Helsinki and discovered a large, sunny room with a bath and small kitchen for rent. A kindly young maid named Rosa served all the apartment residents. "You must take it, Matilda," Helena said. "Pappa is paying for it."

Matilda didn't object. She had been feeling quite tired lately.

A few days after her move, Matilda found a letter from Helena full of home news. It ended with, "Your mailing list now numbers eight thousand names!"

Thanks be to God, Matilda thought. *Heikki's family will make eight thousand and one.*

Another letter was from an ex-convict.

Do you remember years ago when you first began to visit Vasa Prison? In Cell No. 8 you spoke kindly to a boy of seventeen who was there for manslaughter. You gave him a New Testament. I am that boy! I served five years in Kakola Prison and have been a free man for years. I am rich now. I have a big house with a guest room and farm. The room is just for you, whenever you want to visit. I will drive you around to all the villages and you can teach the people about God and His salvation. Please write at once. What would have happened to that seventeen-year-old boy if someone had not cared for his soul? I can never thank you enough.

Matilda circled the date on her calendar. It would be good to see her friend again.

Early the next morning the maid knocked on her door. "Someone named Eric wishes to see you, Miss," she announced.

"Please show him in," said Matilda. Eric had spent time at Sornas Prison for thievery and was now free. He was very young, but about as energetic as a mummy, preferring thievery to honest work.

Matilda shook his hand and they sat at her desk. "How is it with you, Eric?"

He couldn't face her. "I still find things," he stammered. "Things that don't belong to me. I just find them in my hand somehow, and people misunderstand. I can't help it, Miss Wrede, I have a disease. It's called klepto- — klepto-something."

"Kleptomania?"

"Yes. Alas, that's what I have." He eyed her slyly.

"What a tragic thing," Matilda exclaimed, "that folks might actually think you are stealing. Do you have any warning for the mood that comes over you?"

"About an hour."

"I believe I see the solution to your disease. If you feel an attack coming on, run quickly to my room here. If I am out, look for a key under the doormat. Take anything you wish, but don't touch my papers on the desk. They are of no value to anyone but me. When you feel better, you can return the items. I will understand it is only your disease —which you cannot help," she added with a twinkle in her eye.

Eric promised to fight against his impulses to steal. He also promised to get a full-time job and stay out of trouble.

"I believe you," Matilda said.

The next morning, as Matilda prepared to visit Matti, she heard a knock on her door. Armas staggered in, reeking of beer. He was in his forties with a hilly complexion and a nose like a garlic bulb.

"I'm working, Miss Wrede, indeed I am, every day since I got out of prison."

"I'm proud of you," Matilda said as Armas lunged into her rocking chair. "Do you put money in the bank?"

"Almost every penny," he said. "I put my money into the big brewery bank, the best there is."

Matilda stamped her foot. "You mean you spend it all on drink?"

"Yes, Miss, I must have a drop now and then. But I kept my promise. I promised to come and confess to you whenever I felt weak and gave in to drink. And here I am, to confess."

"You're not sober now."

"No, Miss Wrede. If I were sober, I wouldn't have the courage to come and face you and confess. So I had to get drunk first."

Matilda didn't know whether to laugh or cry. "I could help you open a joint account with me at my bank," she said. "I will trust you with the bank book and I will put a little money in from time to time, just for emergencies. Would you like that?"

His face reddened. "I will try very hard to live up to trust like that," he said.

After Armas left, Matilda walked to Katajanokka Prison, where Matti was now confined. She stopped at Onni's cell first to say hello to him. While they were talking, the guard knocked at the wooden door. "Pardon, Miss Wrede, but Vaino in Cell No. 5 wishes to see you right away."

"Excuse me, Onni," Matilda said. "I think Vaino just wants a copy of my newsletter. I'm ashamed to say I forgot him last time." She dropped her cloak on the pallet and went to Cell No. 5.

"Well, now, friend Vaino, what is the hurry, eh?"

The gentle man looked up from drawing on his slate. "I just wanted to make sure I got a copy of your newsletter this time," he said. "If there's not enough to go around I don't want to be left out again."

"I am sorry about that," Matilda said, handing him one. "Was there no way to borrow a copy?"

"Oh, no. No prisoner would ever give up one of your letters."

Matilda smiled. "So, what have you there on your slate?"

Vaino held up the drawing. He had sketched a fish, but only the head and tail had flesh and scales. The body was bony skeleton. "This is you, Miss Wrede. You are still alive, thank God, but your body is wearing out. Please take care of yourself, for our sakes." He handed her the drawing.

She thanked him, then returned to Onni's cell. Her cloak sat neatly folded on the pallet.

"Your coat fell on the floor," Onni said. "When I brushed it off your purse fell out and the clasp opened. I put the purse back in your pocket."

"Thank you," Matilda said, putting on her cloak. "I will visit again next week and stay longer."

"Aren't you going to count your money?"

"Why should I? No one else but you has been in here."

Onni's face showed his concern. "But I am a thief."

"My purse has been as safe with you as it would have been with me."

Onni's voice shook and his hands trembled. "Oh, Miss Wrede, to think you have faith in me after all the evil I've done."

Matilda smiled and walked to Matti Haapoja's cell.

"Miss Wrede! Oh, how I've longed to see you." He gripped her small hand in his powerful one, a peaceful expression on his face. "I have applied to the public prosecutor and asked him to send me back to Siberia."

Matilda's heart almost stopped. "Siberia? Why?"

"I confessed to more crimes I committed there. An innocent person would have been executed in Siberia for my crimes if I hadn't given testimony of the truth. Now that I am God's child, I must make things right in my life."

Matilda said nothing. She heard the guard's ominous footsteps pacing in the hall. She felt the cold, clinging dampness of the cell and smelled its raw, rooty odor. She sat beside Matti on the pallet. "Of course you must," she said. She knew her words had a hollow ring. This was the end of her hopes for a pardon for him. He had been changed, rehabilitated. But now that he had confessed to more crimes, what hope was there?

Matilda remained quiet, and Matti mistook her silence for fatigue. "You work too hard for us prisoners," he said. "You will wear out, and then what will happen to us?"

"Do not fear," Matilda said, even though he was expressing her own deepest concern. "God will provide."

"Now that you are here," Matti said, "there is one favor I wish to ask. There are crimes in my past I have never admitted to anyone. I feel a need to confess to some righteous person. Can you bear to listen?"

Matilda stifled the sigh that began deep in her heart. "If it will help you, I will listen." Was that not the main need of a prisoner, to have someone listen?

She wasn't prepared for what followed. Matti told of his early life, how his sister Tarja had worked at menial jobs to educate him, how she did without clothing and sometimes food to send him money. She hated her job in Tavastehus Prison. She had longed to be a teacher. But she sacrificed her dreams for his.

His dream was to sail around the world, for Finnish sailors were sure of a job with any shipping country. Sometimes a sailor was gone for years. There were many temptations. Life on shipboard became Matti's downfall.

"They gave us grog to drink and I soon developed a taste for it. There was no pure water on board. At every port, I went ashore and did whatever I pleased."

He described in detail the most atrocious deeds. Matilda froze in horror and gripped the edge of the pallet. He talked for over two hours.

When Matti stopped speaking he seemed greatly relieved. "If I am to die for my crimes," he said, "it will be just. Do you think they will grant the last wish of a man condemned to death?"

"I believe that is the custom," Matilda said softly.

"My last wish is for you to be with me when I die. I can't abide the chaplains and the parsons. Will you be there?"

"I will insist on it," Matilda said. "But Haapoja, you must not give up hope. I am praying for a miracle."

"No miracles," he said. "I have confessed to man and God, and justice must be done." He stood. "Now, I have a surprise. I am going to invite you to dinner. I see you hardly take time to eat. You are no bigger than one of the starveling birds in winter." He showed her a mug of skimmed milk and a small piece of butter on a folded sheet of newspaper. "I earned a few pennies of my own, and the warden was able to purchase a half-penny's worth of milk and a half-penny's worth of butter. When he gave me my slab of sour rye bread this morning, I opened the

Bible you gave me and asked him to lay the bread upon it. I would not touch the bread you would eat with my bloodstained hands."

Matilda accepted the food and drink, weeping bitterly as she ate.

Was this God's answer to her prayers for Matti? *Sorry, no miracles available today.*

21

GOOD-BYE, MY REIMA

A few weeks later, Pekonen, a young locksmith Matilda had met in prison, came to her apartment. He had big, bony shoulders that almost touched his ears.

"No one will hire an ex-convict," he told her. "I want to go where I'm not known. If I could get to America somehow, I'd start all over and live a good life. Do you think you could help me, Miss Wrede?"

"I have very little money," she said, "and I don't own anything of value. However, let's pray about it and see what God does."

After he left, she thought of something. She did own one thing that was valuable. Reima, her beloved horse. Pappa had given Reima to Matilda on her last birthday, to pull her carriage when she was home. Reima was as dear to Matilda as any friend could be.

But Pekonen was a human being, longing to make a fresh start in America. For days she struggled to smother her conscience. Finally, she took the train back to Rabbelugn to see Reima. Pappa was not at home but Helena came running out to the barn.

"What a splendid idea," Helena said. "Let's go for a ride together."

"I want to ride alone today," Matilda told her. Pekka offered to accompany her, but she politely declined his offer as well.

Matilda headed for the moor and the Ritola farm beyond it. "This will be our last ride," she said, smoothing Reima's mane. When she arrived at the farm, Matilda gave Reima one last carrot, one last apple, and one last hug. Then she pocketed the money she'd received for the horse and asked one of the Ritola servants to drive her home.

When Pekonen returned the next day, he asked, "Did God answer our prayer?"

"He did," said Matilda, showing him the money. "This should pay for your steamer ticket. Meet me here at 2:00 on Friday and we'll go together to the ship's office on the dock."

Pekonen's eyes grew large. "I will never forget how you helped me find a decent life again," he cried.

She watched him go down the street, three quick steps then a shuffle; three more steps then a skip. She was glad she could help him.

On Friday afternoon, rain thundered and the streets turned into rivers of mud.

"You must not go out in this weather," Pekonen said when she answered the door. Rain soaked his cap and rolled down his nose. "It's so blustery out there, and the streets so full of deep rapids, I nearly fell crossing the street. You'd catch your death out there."

"Very well." Matilda placed a small canvas pouch into his hands. "Here is the money. God bless you, Pekonen. Write me the minute you get settled in America."

He thanked her over and over, then went back out into the storm.

The following week many of her prisoner friends were being sent into exile. The convoy would start out from Viborg, on the Russian border, headed for the terrible Nerchinesk mines in Siberia. She had promised to ride with them as far as possible.

Matilda visited the prison. Though it was late summer, an early blizzard locked the city in its icy grip. Leaving her cloak and boots in the waiting room, she visited the prisoners doomed to exile in Siberia. As she hurried down the cold corridor she bumped into the Chief Inspector of Prisons.

"Miss Wrede, what a pleasure to see you again. Why, where is your cloak? You are shivering and positively blue with cold."

"I can't visit my friends dressed in warm clothes," she replied. "The men are freezing in their cells. They might envy my wool cloak and warm boots and not pay attention to my message."

He stared at her a moment, shook his head, then

walked away. Matilda overheard the prisoners exclaim to one another, "She would rather freeze than wear her coat and boots. She does this for us."

On the day before the convoy left, Matilda bade each prisoner farewell. She felt deeply the pain of those who were leaving their loved ones and country forever. She was particularly concerned about Lauri, a hardened criminal only twenty-six years old, who had shown no remorse for his crimes. He did not even pretend to be a Christian, and he was often rude to Matilda. Once he spread lies that she had helped a prisoner escape by giving him a file.

"I wish I could ride with you," Matilda exclaimed, "at least as far as Viborg."

"That would be a great comfort for us," Lauri said, "but we would feel ashamed. They are going to shave half of our heads, dress us in striped clothes, and lock us in fetters. Besides, I'm afraid such a trip would affect your health. It's better that we go alone."

The other prisoners agreed, though she could tell it grieved them. Matilda respected their wishes to spare her. At day's end, she walked the long prison corridor to the exit. On every side prisoners held out their hands to her through the cell bars, bidding her a silent, terrible farewell.

The next morning, she changed her mind about riding the prison train. She boarded at Kymmene Station and found Lauri in the prison railway carriage. "I am allowed to ride as far as Kaipias," she said, sitting by him.

Lauri's eyes softened. "You shouldn't ride in a prison car," he said. "People might think you are one of us. There are some women going into exile too."

"I *am* one of you." She pulled a handkerchief out of her pocket and placed it under Lauri's neck iron, to keep it from bruising him.

All too soon, the train chugged into Kaipias. When it stopped, a crowd of nosy villagers gathered around the window to the prisoner's carriage, shouting insults.

"I will fetch you a cup of coffee and be right back," Matilda said. She got off the train and faced the crowd. "Fie!" she cried. "Get along with you. There is nothing here for you to see." No one paid her any heed.

Hurrying back with the hot coffee, she handed it to Lauri. He drank greedily as the insults continued.

"Warden," Matilda called. "Please stand in front of the window so the prisoners cannot be seen." The warden hesitated, but did as she asked. She took Lauri's hand. "I must go now, but I will wire a friend in Viborg. She will have coffee and currant buns ready for all the prisoners."

Lauri's expression changed from ferocious to helpless as he tried to thank her. He looked like a little boy. "Farewell," he said, his voice unsteady. "I will write to you if I am allowed."

The train that would take her back to the city pulled into the station. Matilda boarded it and rode back to Helsinki feeling depressed.

Several weeks later, as Matilda was walking home from the prison late one foggy afternoon, she saw a man ambling down the sidewalk. Three quick steps, then a shuffle. Three more steps, then a skip. And a drunken lurch straight into a tavern.

It looked like Pekonen, but it couldn't be. He was in

America . . . wasn't he? She followed the man into the tavern. It was a dark, dingy place lit only by one lantern on the wall.

She stopped at a table where eight men drank and laughed. She recognized every one of them. "What are you doing here? Is this how you keep your promise to me not to drink?"

"What are *you* doing here, Miss Wrede?" one asked.

"I thought I saw Pekonen come in. The one who emigrated to America."

They burst out in harsh laughter, all pointing to a table in the corner. "Then that must be America," said another of the men.

Matilda groped her way to the corner table. Pekonen sat there, nursing a drink. Matilda slapped the table, interrupting his sulking. "I sold my dearest friend for you. Where is the money I gave you?"

"I have only a few pennies left," said Pekonen meekly.

"Get up." Matilda pulled him by the ear. "Come with me."

He shuffled along after her while the others hooted and jeered.

Matilda led him to her apartment and pushed him into a chair. "Don't you dare move until I come back." She went to the maid's apartment. "Rosa, I need you to make me a cup of your strongest coffee. Mix in spoonfuls of ginger and pepper and mustard. That'll sober up my houseguest."

Rosa laughed. "Yes, Miss, if it don't kill him."

Matilda watched Rosa prepare the brew. The maid was so tall she easily reached the high cupboards containing the requested ingredients. Her long, dark hair was pulled into a neat white cap that matched her maid's uniform. She was a beautiful young woman, and Matilda wondered if the apartment tenants would lose this wonderful maid when some tall, charming man caught her eye and offered to marry her.

Matilda took the steaming mixture back to her apartment. She found Pekonen sound asleep, his feet propped up on her embroidered footstool.

"Wake up," she ordered, "and drink this."

He blinked, sat up, and took the mug. With the first sip, he choked and gasped. "Such a terrible taste."

"Drink up," Matilda demanded, and he drained the cup dry. "How could you do such a terrible thing, and to me who only wished you well?" She told him about Reima. Pekonen shed tears and apologized over and over.

"And now, as a Christian, you must forgive me, mustn't you, Miss Wrede?"

"I suppose so," she said.

He promised to try to earn his own passageway to America, and she let him go.

At the end of the week she received a note from a family friend near Rabbelugn.

My dear Matilda,

I heard about Reima, and I'm sure you had good reasons for selling him. Knowing you, I imagine you needed money for one of your prisoner friends. I have purchased Reima back for you. You may come here any time to ride, or take him back to Rabbelugn.

All the best, Selma.

22

MATILDA MEETS
THE CZAR

The great city of St. Petersburg, Russia, was chosen as the location for the International Prison Congress in 1890. Matilda was invited to attend by Colonel Pashkoff and his wife, who had known the Wrede family for years. The colonel had once been exiled for his faith, but now lived quietly with his wife in a modest home. They invited Matilda to stay with them while she attended the Congress.

"Rosa," said Matilda to the maid, "how would you like to go to Russia with me?"

"Ooh, never, Miss Wrede. Those who go to Russia don't come back."

"I knew you would want to go with me," teased Matilda.

"Why on earth are you going to Russia?" Rosa dusted the sparse furniture in the room.

Matilda explained about the Congress. "I have been asked to be a delegate and represent Finland on behalf of prisoners."

"And why do you want me to go?" she asked, feigning disinterest.

"It would be such a help to have a companion. Besides, nobody would bother two strong women like us," Matilda teased again.

"You hardly weigh a pound," Rosa countered with a smile. "I make up for it, though. I wouldn't say I'm overly heavy, but I am quite a handful."

"I made arrangements to pay the apartment manager for your time off," Matilda went on. "Now, don't look so astonished. I will pay you, also, so you will suffer no financial loss. We will stay in my friend's lovely home. We shall meet the czar himself, and many other royal persons. Queen Olga of Greece, the Empress Marie, Prince Vladimir, ministers of state and foreign ambassadors. Oh, Rosa, please say yes."

The maid sat on the edge of the wide window seat. "The czar! He is the greatest jailer in the world. He holds the key to the ice dungeon of Siberia. Many Finns have died there."

"True. But we are not going as prisoners. We will be his guests."

"Do you speak Russian, Miss Wrede?"

"No. But the Russian nobility only speak it to their servants. French will be the language spoken at the

Congress. I remember enough to understand and speak it fairly well."

"Let me pack your clothes," Rosa said. She opened Matilda's wardrobe, finding only two black dresses. "Why, Miss Wrede, where are your ball gowns? You'll need two or three, won't you?"

Matilda laughed. "I will be a little dark hen among the birds of paradise."

"And your jewels, Miss? Won't they need polishing?"

"I have only this," Matilda said, pointing to her collar. "My 'Grace and Peace' pin is of far more value than any gem. So, Rosa, have you decided? Please say you'll go with me."

Rosa pretended to think it over, then jumped up. "Of course I'll go," she squealed. "Serving tea, making beds, and dusting all day does get tiresome. Besides, I think I'll like Russia. New food, new scenery, outings with the other servants, no doubt."

"I'm sure they'll treat you well."

"Do you think I'll get a peek at the fine gentry? I could hide behind a heavy drape at the ball with just my nose showing."

Matilda laughed at the image. "I'll ask if you may assist the maids who serve food at the reception," she said. "You'll have to learn Russian customs and ways."

"It sounds positively delightful."

Colonel Pashkoff and his wife welcomed Matilda and Rose to St. Petersburg. After the women were settled in guest rooms, the colonel's wife loaned Matilda a soft maroon ball gown and a matching lace shawl. "I suppose I would be too conspicuous in black," Matilda said. "So I won't embarrass you, I'll wear it." But she still clasped her "Grace and Peace" pin to the collar.

The Congress was held in the magnificent Hall of the Nobles. Czar Nicholas II himself made the opening remarks. He stood tall and straight, with dark hair and sideburns. He wore a military uniform with gold trim and medals.

Matilda thought that being in the Hall of Nobles was like standing inside a jewelry box lined with red and gold satin. The guests looked like living jewels in colors more dazzling than rainbows. The women sparkled like diamonds, or glowed like rich-blooded rubies, or flashed by in emerald hues. The men wore dress swords with silver decorations.

That night, Rosa brushed Matilda's hair and demanded to know everything that had happened. Matilda eagerly shared the details.

"I'm so glad I came along," Rosa chattered. "I helped in the bakery today, and what delicious goodies you will have for dinner tomorrow night. One of the bakery boys smiles at me all the time. It wouldn't be proper to smile back, would it, Miss Wrede?"

"Dear me, no," Matilda said. "It's much too soon. You must know him at least a year."

"Must I really? Or are you just teasing me?"

Matilda laughed. "I have something for you." She handed Rosa a golden box tied with blue silk ribbon. "Bonbons, from the czarina. Everyone received a box. Eat only a few a day. They are very rich."

"Oh, thank you, Miss, thank you."

The next day, Matilda was given a seat of honor in a gilt carriage drawn by four white horses. She toured museums and exhibitions and attended receptions. She admired the art treasures of Russia and dined at a sumptuous country villa.

On the last day of the Congress, Matilda sat in the audience and listened to the head of the Criminal Department of France. He spoke about the prisoners, calling them hopeless cases who had been born bad. "There is no solution but to lock them up," he declared. "Criminals cannot be helped or changed."

Matilda fidgeted uneasily. She was the only one there who represented the prisoners themselves. She must speak up. But she hadn't the faintest idea what to say. She had prepared no speech. *Lord,* she prayed, *you once told me to open my mouth wide and you would fill it. Please do so now.*

As the audience applauded the Frenchman's speech, Matilda rose and made her way to the lectern. All eyes focused on her. She was the only woman at the conference.

The chairman hesitated, then introduced her. "Baroness Matilda Wrede of Finland."

"Gentlemen," she began, speaking French easily, "laws and systems cannot alter the heart of a criminal, but God can. Prisoners can be changed. I have seen it happen. Even those called hopeless cases can be transformed by the power of God. I am convinced that we must care about the prisoners' souls and their spiritual lives. In this way convicts can become good citizens."

As she returned to her seat, applause rose all around her. After the meeting was adjourned, many audience members thanked her for her courage. Not one of the other delegates had even mentioned God or Christianity as having any part in changing a prisoner.

Back in her rooms, Matilda found Rosa bursting with excitement. She twirled around the room on tiptoe with a bedspread wrapped around her shoulders like a ball gown. "Oh, Miss, I saw them. The colonel loaned me a maid's uniform and I walked into one of the dinners carrying a little tray of radishes and placed it by a lady's plate. Then I curtseyed and walked out so sedately. Did you see me?"

"I did," said Matilda. "I held my breath lest you drop the tray, but you were a credit to Finland."

"Oh, you're teasing me again. A gentleman at the table noticed me and smiled. Should I have smiled back?"

"I hope you did no such thing," Matilda said. "Your place was to lower your eyes and walk away. Besides, what about the baker's boy?"

"Who? Oh . . . him." Rosa threw the bedspread onto a chair and slumped into the window seat. "Miss Wrede, be honest with me. Could a servant girl like me ever marry into the gentry? I do so love chocolates and ball gowns and dancing and parties."

Matilda stifled the gentle laugh that rose in her throat. "All this gaiety belongs to Russia. When you get home, you will remember that you are Finnish. And now, Rosa, I need you to pack our things. We will be leaving sooner than I thought."

"But tonight is the banquet at the czar's winter palace," cried Rosa. "You told me you would have a place of honor at the Imperial Table. Won't you stay for that?"

"No. The colonel will be upset, but I've had quite enough of feasting. Besides, a spy has been following me."

Rosa's mouth dropped open. "A spy! After you, Miss Wrede? Or me?"

"Just me. He is an agent, though I don't know for whom. He asked me why I ride free with my railroad pass. How would he know that? He asked about Finland's political prisoners. He posed personal questions about Colonel Pashkoff as well. For the colonel's sake, we must leave right away."

Rosa fell silent. "Are you in danger, Miss Wrede?"

"No," Matilda said. "But our country may be."

23

MATTI HAAPOJA

Baron Carl Gustav Wrede died on July 18, 1892. Sweet Pappa, who had sympathized with Matilda's prison work once he saw the hand of God in it. Wise Pappa, her guide and counselor. Generous Pappa, who had made it possible for her to travel the rails and visit Lapland and the lake country.

Rabbelugn was sold and the money divided among the baron's nine children. Helena went to live with one of the married brothers. Matilda banked her share and drew from it sparingly. After the funeral Matilda told her sister, "I must return to prison work right away. That will occupy my mind and keep me from missing Pappa."

She found a room near Kakola Prison where she could stay while she visited her convict friends. A week later, as she was leaving the prison, a sudden chest pain hit her and she sought out the prison doctor. He listened to her heart. Seating her comfortably on a chair in the courtyard, he said, "Stay here. Don't move. I'm going to call a carriage for you."

"What's wrong?" Matilda asked.

"You've had a heart attack, and it could be quite serious."

Matilda rested in the sunshine. The prisoners gathered around, their faces full of worry. They talked in low tones among themselves.

Finally, an old man came up to her from the group. "Miss Wrede, you taught us that God is love, that He knows our thoughts and can do anything. He must know that you are the only friend we have. If He loves us as you say, how could He take our only friend away from us? If you die, I think we would all hate Him." The other men looked at her, nodding.

Matilda took shallow breaths to ease the pain. How could she answer them? "If I die," she said, "it will be your fault."

The men looked at each other.

"God knows you love me too much," she explained. "Perhaps you love me even more than you love God. If He sees that I am in the way, He might take me so that you will give your best love to Him. So, you see, it is up to you whether I live or die."

She closed her eyes and rested while the men stood all around her like an honor guard. When the carriage arrived, two of the strongest carried her chair to the gate.

For eight months, Matilda stayed with Helena and

their brother's family. Then she took a vacation in Kremonin Castle in Livonia, a small Russian province near Estonia, with a friend of the family, Princess Liewen. The princess loaned Matilda a pair of lively ponies and a cart to explore the charming countryside. After two months of this, Matilda declared herself cured.

She heard that Matti Haapoja had finally been transferred to Tavastehus Prison, so she rented a room in town and asked to visit him.

"Miss Wrede," the prison governor said, "I'm afraid you cannot see him. He was wounded while trying to escape."

"Escape?" Matilda felt the blood drain from her face. "He would never try to do that. He is a changed man."

"Nevertheless, he did. He became angry when the public prosecutor refused to allow him to return to Siberia to give testimony. He hid a shoemaker's knife in his shirt." The governor paused. "Based on *your* recommendation, Miss Wrede, the prisoners were allowed to exercise in the courtyard. Matti used the knife to grip a wall that was crumbling, and he climbed almost to the top. He almost escaped, Miss Wrede."

Matilda stared at him, trying to imagine the horrible scene.

"Then," the governor continued, "he wounded the warden and tried to stab himself to death."

"Oh, no!" Matilda gripped the chair edge.

"He punctured his heart. He lives, which is a miracle if ever I saw one. But a rather dubious miracle, if you ask me."

"I must see him," Matilda cried. "Please."

The governor frowned. "As you wish," he said. "But

don't get too near him. And don't trust him. He is a violent man."

Matilda found Matti lying on a straw mat on the cold floor. When he saw her, he tried to pull his blanket up to hide the iron ring around his neck. "Forgive the way I look," he muttered.

Matilda knelt by him, not saying a word.

"I couldn't bear it any longer," he said. "The public prosecutor did not keep his word. Why do they expect prisoners to keep their word when others are so false? An innocent person in Siberia is going to be executed because of me." He breathed hard. Flecks of blood stained his lips.

Matilda held his big hand in both of hers.

"They will hang me now. But I don't want you to be present. I heard about your heart attack. You must not see me die. I would rather kill myself than give you pain."

Matilda sat on the floor beside him. "Don't even think of such an awful thing. I'll visit you every day and we'll have a Bible reading and a hymn and a prayer. God will help you recover."

"Not this time." He turned his face to the wall and closed his eyes. Matilda stood. "Please come again, my dearest friend."

Matilda hurried to the office of the prison governor. "Why isn't Matti Haapoja in the prison hospital?" she asked the startled secretary. The woman shrugged as if to say, *Why bother? He deserves to die.*

Matilda stormed out of the prison and stomped back to her room, where she spent a sleepless night praying for

Matti. As soon as the prison doors opened in the morning, she entered. In the office she found Tarja, Matti's sister.

"It is good to see you again, Tarja," Matilda said. "I hope you have been well."

Tarja glared at her.

"I'm here to see Matti," Matilda said. "He asked me to visit."

"Are you happy with what you've accomplished?" Tarja asked, black with fury and desperately fighting back her grief.

"Tarja, what's the matter?" Matilda asked.

"You don't know, do you? Matti's dead. And it's your fault."

"He can't be." Matilda swayed and leaned against the wall.

"He is." Tarja twisted her reddened fingers. "And by his own hand. You stirred up his conscience, telling him to go back to Siberia and confess to more crimes. You killed him, I tell you."

"I don't understand," Matilda whispered. "For God's sake, Tarja, tell me what happened."

"He plunged a knife into his heart again. This time he died."

"I don't believe you," she sobbed. "Let me see him."

"Impossible. They've taken the body away." Tarja bawled like a child, pounding her fists together.

Matilda sank into a chair by the desk, put her head down, and wept. After a few minutes, she sat up and wiped her face. "Tarja, I didn't even know of any crimes he committed in Siberia. That was his idea. He had such a change of heart and faith in God that he wanted his conscience clear."

Tarja threw herself into the chair across from Matilda. "He was all I had on earth. I lived for him. He had a wonderful beginning in life. He could have been anything. Anything."

Matilda opened her purse and took out a letter that had been folded and refolded many times. "He wrote me this when I was convalescing from a heart attack. I'd like to read it to you." Without waiting for a response, she read.

Dear Matilda Wrede, sister in the Lord Jesus Christ,

Thank you for your letters. They are so full of a beautiful spirit, I cry when I read them. Our loving heavenly Father said, "The good shepherd gives His life for the sheep." And you keep giving your life for us prisoners. You have awakened the yearning after God that slumbered in our hearts. You have come to teach His Word to miserable, wretched creatures who had no hope of forgiveness or heaven. We still need you. God will not let you die of your heart trouble. All the prisoners' voices here are lifted up in prayer for you, dear sister. As for my own life, it goes on quietly from day to day through the grace of a living Savior, Jesus Christ, to whom be glory forever.

Your friend, Matti Haapoja.

Matilda refolded the letter. "That is how I will remember him. I hope it will comfort you, also, Tarja. We must leave with God what we cannot understand."

Tears spilled over Tarja's lumpy cheeks as she reached out a hand. Matilda cried in sympathy for this unhappy woman.

24

PRISON DOORS CLOSE

Matilda was more than glad to return to her apartment in Helsinki. After a few days' rest, she visited a prisoner in Kakola named Esko. He was serving a ten-year sentence for murdering his sister-in-law and had asked to speak to "the angel of the prisons."

Matilda found the young farm worker repentant and sincere. His face was still tanned from outdoor life.

"Our family was respected all through the district," he told her, "and that made what I did even more horrifying. In the busy hay-making time of late summer, I caught a fever from an infection. I could hardly breathe. I kept working as long as I could. But finally, I took to bed. My brother's wife, Ana, nagged at me for going to bed and letting the relatives do all the work. She thought I was just being lazy."

Matilda shook her head.

"I couldn't stand, and Ana refused to bring me water or food. My fever rose so high I became confused and delirious. One night I got up out of bed and killed her."

Matilda gasped.

"When I realized what I had done, I immediately went to the authorities and confessed. I will spend ten years in this terrible place without a glimpse of sky or grass or a breath of fresh air. My brother hates me. I wrote a letter telling my family how sorry I am for what I did, but I have not been allowed to send it."

Matilda recalled a farmstead she'd visited during her trip to the lake country. The farmer and his wife had talked about their son, Esko, who was in prison.

"When we sent our little ones to school," the mother had said, "we used to give them a baked potato or a hard roll or an egg to eat on the way. Now I want to send my son some food for his hard life's journey." She had written down some Bible verses and asked Matilda if she would take them to him. "He is in God's school now and I pray all day he may learn the lessons God has for him. Then he will be rich in wisdom when he comes back."

Matilda searched in her purse and handed the list of verses to Esko. "Since you are not allowed to send your letter, perhaps you could give it to me and I will see it reaches your parents."

Esko tried to thank Matilda, but broke into a fevered spasm of coughing.

"You should be in the prison hospital," she said, standing. "I will speak to the doctor right now."

The small hospital was filled to overflowing with sick men. Beds were crammed next to each other. Several of the men moaned, "Water. Just a sip, for the love of God."

Matilda stopped by one bed and saw that a man's broken arm had not been set. The bone showed through an open wound. Another man was covered with crusty sores. Bedbugs twitched about in the dirty blanket under him. None of the prisoners appeared to have been fed or washed.

She stepped into the cubicle that was the doctor's office. No one was there. She ran to the prison governor's office. "Have you seen the hospital?" she asked. "The sick men are horribly neglected. You must send workers to help them at once."

"At once?" The governor raised his eyebrows. "We have no one here who can help. And we cannot pay outsiders to work among patients. They fear contagion."

"You are letting them die," Matilda accused.

He shrugged. "They are prisoners."

"The man in Cell 47 is sick with a fever. He needs medicine."

"Esko? He is a murderer."

Matilda headed for the warden's office. "Ilmari," she complained, "the men in the hospital are not being taken care of. Can you do anything?"

His blue eyes were full of sympathy. "Miss Wrede, I'm just a warden. I can't leave my patrol in the corridor."

"Can you get Esko some medicine for fever? I'm afraid he may have tuberculosis."

"No, Miss. No one is allowed to take medicine from the doctor's closet. I'm sorry."

"Where is the doctor?"

"I don't know." Ilmari swallowed hard. "I could take Esko some extra water."

Matilda thanked him quickly and hurried on to the chaplain's office. Rev. Poso rose to greet her, but she refused his offer of a chair.

"I am distressed at the conditions in this prison's hospital. Esko, in Cell 47, is sick with fever but receives no medical attention. He has not been allowed to send letters home. And the food is atrocious. How can prisoners be healthy when they are fed only watery cabbage soup and a bite of bread? Men should not be chained by the neck to the wall, no matter what they have done." She stopped to catch her breath and realized she was sobbing.

"My dear Miss Wrede," the chaplain said, "do calm yourself so we can talk things over."

"No." Matilda turned away. "I'm tired of talking to you people." She buttoned her coat and stormed out of the prison, taking a trolley to the office of the Chief Inspector of Prisons for all of Finland.

The unfriendly receptionist she'd encountered at her previous visit scoffed at her again. And the Chief Inspector's face was just as pink as when she had seen him last. Once again they listened in astonishment.

"I'm asking for an investigation of all the prisons in Finland," Matilda declared. "I have been visiting them for years and conditions are appalling. Men lie in filthy, cold cells in body irons from neck to ankles. All day long, they lie there with nothing to do or think about. I want you to send inspectors immediately."

The receptionist snorted. "I said no good would come of letting her—"

The Chief Inspector silenced her with a glare. "No one asked you. Hold your tongue if you value your job." He turned to Matilda. "I will see what can be done, Miss Wrede."

"Everyone says the same thing," Matilda cried. "You all say you will see what can be done. And nothing is done." She shut the door with a hard push and stomped down the street. She had seen and heard so much and prayed so hard for so long, and still prisoners were treated cruelly.

Well, there was one last thing she could do. She shrank from it, but saw no other way. If good Christian people only knew of conditions behind the stone walls, certainly they would demand reform. She headed for the office of Dr. Gustav Mattson, a well-known journalist. He was eager to interview the famous Matilda Wrede. Even the Siberian colonists had heard of her.

Matilda talked to him for hours and he scribbled page after page of notes. Every time she paused, he lifted his pen and waited for more. Matilda told the story of years of visiting wretched prisoners who were kept locked up under inhuman conditions. She told him everything, even about the prison hospital.

The article was published in a leading Finnish journal. After that, Matilda could not walk the streets without strangers stopping her and sympathizing with her. Just as she hoped, the public was now up in arms, demanding an investigation into the prisons.

She waited a week for the excitement to die down, then visited the prison in Kakola to see Esko. The prison governor was cool to her. "I am sorry," he said, "but you are no longer welcome in my home." In a forced and awkward speech, he added, "Prison visits may be made now only in the presence of the prison governor. This rule has been made because of your . . . religious interfering."

"I would not dream of asking a prisoner to open his heart and talk about his personal feelings with a third person present," she said.

The governor narrowed his eyes. "I think you will find this is true now of all prisons."

"Then my visits must cease. I ask only that you let me see the prisoner Esko for a brief moment."

The governor almost smiled. "He died in his cell two days ago," he said, "of tuberculosis."

25

THE VILLAIN, BOBRIKOFF

Now that I have been cut off from visiting prisoners," Matilda wrote in her diary, "my heart has been opened to others. For all men and women are prisoners until they have been set free by Christ's love."

She kept her door unlocked for any who needed help or wanted to talk. One day a stranger knocked on the door. His mouth was twisted. "I am obliged to wander the streets in the cold weather while you sleep in a warm bed," he seethed. "Is that Christianity, Miss Wrede?"

Matilda gave him enough money to pay for a week's lodging at a room in town. In an hour he was back. He shoved the money into her hand.

"I cannot take this. I only wanted it for liquor. I cannot cheat a person who trusts me so."

Prisoners began sending her gifts. A murderer in Sornas Prison carved a penholder from a broken broom handle. "This broom was used to sweep dirt from prison floors for eighteen years," he wrote. "I carved this penholder for you to remind you to write many letters to us. Please sweep our souls clean, Miss Wrede."

Another convict sent her a paperweight for her desk, a fallen log with a broken ax in it. "The log is the prisoner's heart," his note explained. "The ax that has broken the wood is the love of God. The handle is broken, for your frail body has been broken from your unceasing toil for us."

Voivo sent her a wooden spoon with a dandelion painted on it. His letter explained, "In the prison yard we all watched a brave little green plant growing between two stones. We were all careful not to step on it, as it was the only green thing we could see. Finally it put out a bud, then a flower like a little golden sun. How we all loved that plant. Then it went to seed and became a ball of fluff, which a breeze blew all over the prison yard, to sow itself into every crack where there was a speck of dirt."

Matilda had to wipe a tear from her eye before she could continue.

"That dandelion is like you, Miss Wrede. You dared to come among sinful prisoners, into uncleanness and sorrow. You have sown the seeds of God's Word in Kakola and we are better men because of it."

On Voivo's birthday, Matilda trudged through deep

snow and fierce wind to visit him. One of her boots was worn through and her foot became soaked and chilled by the time she returned.

That night she ran a fever and became delirious. Her room was to be filled with potted plants, on window sills, in corners, and on the night table. They looked like prisoners on their way to exile in Siberia.

"My dear friends," she cried out. "Here I have been lying comfortably in bed while you stand for hours. I'll get up so you can rest here for a while."

She sprang out of bed, then immediately fainted. She lay on the cold linoleum floor all night. The next day Rosa found her and called a doctor, who came and examined her.

He told her she had developed severe lung trouble. "You will not get better on a diet such as yours. Why, Rosa tells me you eat only a few vegetables and hardly any milk or eggs."

"I live simply, like the prisoners," Matilda said from her rocking chair near the window.

"Well, you certainly are mad," he exclaimed, then added, "Of course, the world could use a few more mad people such as you."

Her door remained open to all. A dock worker, newly released from prison, came to wish her well as she convalesced. He had been drinking and held on to the bedpost as he towered over her. "You are very ill," he said solemnly.

Matilda couldn't resist smiling. "My heavenly Father knows I can't spare the time to die."

"Where do you plan to be buried?"

"With my family, behind a little stone church in Anjala."

"I would enjoy going there on Sunday afternoons," he said. "I could sit and chat with you."

Matilda tried to hide her smile. "Would you come nice and proper, or would you bring a bottle along?"

He raised his hand to heaven. "Never a bottle on your grave," he vowed.

Matilda slowly recovered, but her sufferings continued. Her beloved sister Helena died. Scarcely had she recovered from this great loss when a dictator seized control of Finland. A Russian named Nikolai Bobrikoff became the new Governor General of Finland and tried to crush the freedoms of the people. His spies were everywhere. He destroyed twenty-two newspapers, banishing the editors to Siberia. He censored all books. He abolished the Finnish army. Then he attacked freedom of religion. His sole desire seemed to make sure Finland became completely Russian.

Matilda grieved for her country. She asked God to help her know what she could do. Once day, while reading in her rocking chair, she remembered being introduced to Archbishop Antonius when he was dedicating a Russian Church that had been built in Finland. He had shown great concern for prisoners—indeed, for all oppressed people.

"If ever I can be of service to you in any way," he had said, "I will certainly do so."

The archbishop was now head of the Russian Church in St. Petersburg. Matilda decided to go there and ask him to speak to the czar about the injustices done to Finland by Nikolai Bobrikoff. She asked Rosa if she would be willing to help with her secret plan.

"Of course," the maid replied without hesitation.

"You can say nothing to anyone," Matilda said.

"I promise," Rosa replied, eyeing the black clothes Matilda had laid out on the bed. "Did someone very important die?"

"Our country is dying, Rosa. That is why I am wearing full mourning garb. But with God's help, someone might save it."

Rosa pulled Matilda's tattered traveling bag out of the closet and laid it on the bed. "How will you ever see through that heavy black veil?"

"You must ask me no questions," Matilda said softly. "Now, take your little scissors and cut out all the name tags from my clothing. Bonnet, coat, dress, shoes, petticoat. All name tags must be snipped out."

"Even . . . ?" Rosa burst into giggles.

"All marks of identification," Matilda snapped. "My life could depend upon it."

Rosa's twittering ceased. "Are you going on a spy mission?"

"No," said Matilda. "But there will be spies around, no doubt." If Bobrikoff discovered her plan, Matilda knew she would be arrested, denounced as a traitor, and sent to Siberia.

Matilda traveled to St. Petersburg alone and stayed with a family friend, Baroness Nicolay.

"Archbishop Antonius lives in the Alexander Nevsky Monastery," the baroness said. "My son will drive you there tomorrow. Antonius is never seen in public, and we fear for him."

Their carriage bumped over rutted, winding roads, past three cemeteries and several chapels, before arriving at the monastery. Matilda and Baron Nicolay entered the huge stone building and were shown into a magnificent but empty reception room. She gave her calling card to a servant. "Matilda Wrede, Finland," it read. No title.

Antonius soon appeared. He, too, wore the black robes of mourning. His thin, noble face was lined with sorrow and his hair had turned white. He bowed to her. "Baroness," he murmured so the servant would not hear. "Come into my study." Matilda and the young baron sat at the archbishop's desk as he heated tea in a samovar and filled a plate with plain rolls.

"Honored sir," Matilda began, "I beseech you to speak to the czar on behalf of Finland. Nikolai Bobrikoff is a villain. He encourages uprisings just so he can put them down in the most ruthless ways. He stirs up trouble among the worst sort of people throughout the nation. He bribes released prisoners to do his deeds. These ex-convicts cannot find any other work, so they agree. Bobrikoff also wants the churches under his control. He is an evil tyrant. His spies are everywhere to report anyone who speaks against him. I fear for Finland, sir."

Antonius motioned them both to lean closer. "I am a prisoner here in my own monastery," he whispered. "There are godless forces abroad in Russia. I cannot go and come as I like. The servants spy on me. Espionage is everywhere.

But you have my promise. I will ask for an audience with the czar and beseech him on behalf of Finland."

Matilda thanked him and left. For weeks she waited anxiously for news from Antonius.

One day an old man she had known in Kakola Prison surprised her with a visit. His clothes were shabby and wrinkled, but his smile was almost youthful. "For twenty years I have not touched drink," he told her. "I am a happy family man. I came to know God through you, and I have traveled all this way to thank you. You brought the peace of God into my life when I was an unhappy prisoner."

Later that week a florist delivered an armload of flowers to Matilda. "I am in Helsinki for the day," the attached card read. "I was one of your prisoners, and now I own a hotel in Berlin. Please visit me if you ever get the chance."

That night a note was quietly slipped under the door by a friend of Antonius. "Mission failed. I am so sorry. Trust in God."

26

BOLSHEVISTS FOR BREAKFAST!

Bobrikoff's rule ended abruptly in 1904 when he was assassinated. Scarcely had the country begun to recover from his tyranny when World War I broke out. Finnish men and horses were sent to the front in Russia, under the leadership of Russian officers. Even Matilda's own horses were commandeered. Confused at the Russian orders bawled at them, the animals turned to her with wild eyes.

"Oh, my poor pets," Matilda said to them in Finnish. "The terrible sights you will see. The suffering you will endure in that strange land." She fed them carrots and spoke to them in the only language they understood. They whinnied in response. But the brief farewell ended quickly, and Matilda watched in helpless agony as her dear friends were taken away.

Matilda could not sleep, picturing the suffering of widows and orphans of war. Then something worse than dictatorship or a world war happened. The thing she had sensed when she attended the Prison Congress at St. Petersburg. Revolution. Civil war. Brother against brother.

The Bolshevik Revolution began with Russian workers and soldiers against the czar and his ministers. Because Finland bordered on Russia, the revolt spread across Matilda's beloved country.

When Rosa's uncle was killed in a skirmish in the city, she moved in with Matilda. "I don't understand any of this." Rosa wept on Matilda's shoulder. "Some folks are called Whites and others are called Reds. What does it mean?"

"Names mean nothing," Matilda assured her, "but I will explain what people have invented. Those who favor a Communist state are called Reds. They are seizing power and possessions by force and taking revenge. The gentry who do not favor any change are called Whites. They were born into a title and a comfortable life. If the Whites had helped the peasants of Russia and the needy more, we would not have revolution."

"Which am I?" Rosa asked. "Which are you?"

"I am considered a White," Matilda explained. "But the peasants and common people are my friends. The prisoners I've worked for all my life are also among the Reds."

As Matilda's countrymen fell victim to the horrors of civil war, eighty thousand Finns were thrown into the very dungeons she had visited. Many were her friends.

Rosa ran into the house one day, her eyes wide with fright. "Miss Wrede! Russian soldiers have broken into Kakola Prison and set the prisoners free. What shall we do? What will happen to us? Since you are a White they may come here after you."

"The prisoners are my friends," Matilda said calmly. "They will not harm me. Now, fetch my cut-glass vase, the one Helena gave me."

Rosa rummaged in the back of the closet. "This thin one?"

"Yes. Now, go to the florist in town and buy one long-stemmed red rose and one white one. I will put them both together in my vase on the table. Examine them daily, and when they fade and droop their petals, you must run to the florist and get two more. Take this." She handed Rosa some money. "I will not take sides. All Finns are brothers and sisters. My door will be open to both Reds and Whites."

One morning, as Rosa carried in Matilda's breakfast on a small tray, they heard a noise. Rosa dashed to the front door then ran back to Matilda, twisting her hands. "Oh, Miss Wrede, three Bolshevists with red armbands have pushed their way into the hall, and there are more outside. They look so fierce and wicked. What shall I do?"

"Why, invite them in," said Matilda. "My door is open to anyone, you know that."

Three men, not much older than twenty, strode into the room. Their expressions were arrogant.

Matilda leaned back in her chair. "Good morning, boys. Caps off, now. You are indoors and in the presence of female company."

The men looked at each other, then reached up and yanked off their caps.

"Now, what can I do for you?" Matilda asked.

"We want money," the taller one said.

Matilda eyed them. "I do have a good-sized amount of money in the house for sick and elderly folk, but you can't have it."

"We're hungry," the shorter, portly man complained.

"I was just about to eat my breakfast. I will gladly share it with you." She lifted the towel from the tray, revealing a small dish of boiled cabbage and a half-slice of bread.

The fellows looked at each other uneasily.

"There's hardly enough here for the four of us." Matilda smiled. "If you come back at suppertime we will have roast potatoes and coffee. Then we will discuss how young, strong men like yourselves can find honest jobs."

The men shuffled their feet. "We've stumbled upon Matilda Wrede," one muttered. "Look at the pin—Grace and Peace. We can't steal anything from her."

"Sorry to bother you, Miss," the other mumbled, then they left quickly, nearly stumbling over each other.

From morning until nightfall, Matilda's apartment was filled with people needing help and advice—wives and mothers of soldiers and released prisoners, who all thought of her as friend, mother, and spiritual advisor.

Once, two Red Guards tried to convert her to their viewpoint. She listened patiently, then turned in her rocking chair and pointed to a painting on the wall of Christ gazing over Jerusalem. "I follow the teachings of that man,

Jesus," she said. "His life's work was to give, until finally He gave His life for us. I see you Reds taking, stealing, and looting. There is a vast difference between your teaching and His. I follow Jesus and always will."

She turned to her little table with the vase. "Both of the roses are beautiful. Each needs water and sun. They live together in peace. The beauty of one complements the other. And I love them both."

They looked at the two roses, then nodded respectfully and left, closing the door softly behind them.

During those dark days of anarchy, Matilda talked to a man she had once known as a prisoner. "My mother was killed by the Whites," he said. "A loving, harmless woman who never hurt anyone." He twisted his cap in his hands, his eyes watering. "They broke into the house and cut her down. And for what? All she owned was a poor little cottage and a cow."

Matilda shook her head. "My nephew was killed by the Reds in a street fight. I mourn for him, but I do not harbor any feelings of hatred." Matilda took his gnarled hand in her own. "Do you know who killed your mother?"

"I do."

"Do you seek revenge?"

"No. That would not bring her back. You taught me to value life, Miss Wrede. I cannot kill."

On Matilda's next visit to Kakola Prison she heard that amnesty had been promised by the Reds to the political prisoners.

"The prison gates swung open," a prisoner told her. "Many of us were tempted to run. But I remembered your teaching and took charge. 'If we escape now,' I told my comrades, 'we might be caught again. We must wait for the amnesty to be official. We must see it in writing first. Then we may leave as free men.'"

There was no fighting or bloodshed at Kakola Prison all through the revolution, but in time the inmates became restless. They sent a letter to Matilda asking her to intercede for them to the Revolutionary Headquarters. This she did, and also wrote letters to the governors of all the prisons.

When at last the prisoners were legally free, many of them became Red Guards. Their new freedom became license to jail all Whites. Teachers, other professionals, even clergymen were thrown into prison without a reason.

Matilda went to the police court to find out how the new prisoners were being treated. "I have some money with me for extra food," she told the Red leader. "Please take it so they will have nourishing meals."

He pushed away the bank notes. "Spend it on something else. The White prisoners are fed well enough. You should be glad they're being punished. One of the prisoners here is responsible for ruining your prison ministry."

Matilda knew he was lying. "The streets are full of violence," she said. "Guns and authority are put into the hands of children. They strut about and give orders. Can't you do something about the crime?"

He looked around to see if anyone was listening. "We are powerless," he said in a low tone. "The criminal element has the upper hand."

The famine grew worse. Hungry people knocked on

Matilda's door every day begging for help. Matilda drew on the small amount of money left in her account at the bank.

One day three men dressed in prison garb, newly released in the amnesty, came to her door asking for lunch. Their hair was uncut and greasy. Matilda recognized them as Ensi, Valio, and Arvo. She served them some nourishing soup.

"I was in prison for fifteen years," Valio said. "Freedom is wonderful. But your visits were even better than freedom, Miss Wrede."

Ensi wiped his mouth. "You will never know how much you mean to me and my family."

"Yes," agreed Arvo. "You have a big family, Miss Wrede. Many, many children."

Matilda served them second helpings of soup. They were so thin, so poor, and she did think of them all as her children. She eased herself out of her rocker and opened her bureau drawer. "This is my bank book," she said. "I am not well and I'm always tired, so I can't get about easily." She handed the bank book to Ensi. "You have a wife and children. I see you need work clothes and boots. You take this to the bank right now and withdraw what you need. Then hand it over to Valio so he can take what he needs. He will give it to Arvo. When you all have enough to cover your needs, return the bank book to me. Please be thrifty, for this money must last me a long while."

Matilda waited all day for her bank book to be returned. Rosa fussed over her at day's end, putting the warming pan between the cold sheets and bringing her a cup of tea. "Oh, Miss, you should not have trusted convicts. It was too soon. The old ways of thieving are still in their brains."

The second day passed, and Matilda began to wonder what had happened. When the third day came and went with no sign of the men, Rosa said nothing but went about her tasks angrily.

At the end of the fourth day, the three men returned.

"How could you cheat Miss Wrede out of her life savings?" Rosa wailed. "What terrible times we live in."

"We're dreadful sorry," Valio said, hanging his head. "But none of us had ever seen a bank book, much less held one right in his own hands. We never dreamed you would trust us so much. We decided each one could hold it in his hands for a whole day."

Ensi crinkled his hat. "I walked all over town, thinking, *I have in my pocket the entire life savings of Matilda Wrede. I can never be anything but an honest man after this.* Then Valio got to hold it in his hands for the second day. And the third day Arvo held the bank book in his hands."

"Nothing like this has ever happened to us, Miss Wrede," said Arvo. "We each drew out only a small amount." He shyly handed her the bank book.

Matilda returned it to her bureau drawer. Out of the corner of her eye she glanced at Rosa. She stood transfixed, her mouth open in astonishment.

27

A LIFE PLACED IN THE HANDS OF GOD

The released political prisoners of Kakola pooled the small amount of money they earned and sent Matilda a silver cup with an inscription: "For her who drained the cup of our sorrow, with gratitude forever."

A wealthy lady, who had somehow escaped the notice of the Red Guard, wrote Matilda a letter. "I have much flour hidden away here. Will you accept some of it?"

"Yes, thank you," Matilda wrote back. "If I may give it to the poor who knock at my door, I accept it gladly."

Back came the reply, "It was to protect the flour from the Reds that I wished to send it."

The flour never arrived.

During the worst of the famine, a friend

in the country sent Matilda two sacks of potatoes. One sack was filled with clean, firm potatoes. The other contained frostbitten, soft spuds beginning to rot.

When an old woman came begging for food, Matilda started to drag the sack of damaged potatoes toward her, then stopped. She returned them to the closet and gave the woman the sack of fresh potatoes.

Matilda was often asked to hide a Red or a White in her home. She refused. "My door is open to all who need sympathy or whatever help I can give. But I can hide no one." Many times she felt lonely and misunderstood, but she never wavered. A red rose and a white rose always lived together in the cut-glass vase.

One day a Red Guard asked to see her. "I spent over thirty years in jail for being a thief, and now I've been assigned to guard a bank." The irony amused Matilda. He presented her with three quarts of milk. "I carried this milk for miles so I could give it to you, Miss Wrede. You have fed so many people, now I shall help feed you."

"Forgive me for asking," she said, "but is the milk paid for?"

"Absolutely. It's honest milk. I would never bring you stolen goods."

Matilda thanked him gratefully. The next day she gave the milk to an unwed mother who came seeking help.

Rosa scolded her. "You needed that milk. You scarcely recover from one illness when another strikes you down. You must eat more."

The revolution finally ended when the Red Government fell. Finland was recognized as an independent country, and a Finnish Republic was established. Law and order reigned. The civil war was called "The War of Liberation," but Matilda called it "The War of Brothers." She would never forget the eighty thousand Finns who'd been jailed and put in concentration camps.

As Matilda sat in the rocker in her sunny room, Rosa came to sit beside her. "What a lot of good you have done all your life," she said wistfully. "Newspaper articles praise you. Your life story is written in journals. Piles of mail arrive each day from those you've helped. You are honored by famous people. You just keep going and never give up. What is your secret, Miss Wrede?"

Matilda smiled at her fondly. "There is no secret. A life placed in the hands of God will be used by God. I didn't choose prison work. I never dreamed of such a thing. I simply opened my heart to the Savior, and when He called me I obeyed."

"A life placed in the hands of God," Rosa repeated reverently.

"My prison work is over now," said Matilda sadly. "I suppose you could say I'm retired."

The sound of scuffling feet was followed by a knock on Matilda's door. A deputation of released political prisoners crowded into her room. They were shabby and unwashed and their gaunt faces showed great strain. "We come with a petition for your return to Kakola Prison," one man declared. "Eight hundred prisoners signed it. We need you back, dear Miss Wrede."

Matilda took the paper. "May I read it in private and think it over?"

The men nodded and filed out. One lingered behind. "We know you have grown aged and ill because of us. But maybe, if you came back, you'd feel young again."

After they left, Matilda studied the names on the petition. The political prisoners had been released, she noticed, but the cells had quickly filled with new criminals.

Is it possible? she thought. *Is God calling me to return?* Then, as clearly as she had first heard it in childhood, a voice in her mind said, "Speak to them of Jesus while yet there is time." She turned to see if Rosa had spoken to her, but the maid was in the kitchen washing dishes.

While Matilda sat wondering, a telegram was delivered to her door. The return address identified it as being from the new Chief of All Prisons, whose office was in Helsinki. "I beg you to take up your work again," he wrote. "You are needed now more than ever."

Matilda's pulse raced. *If God has called me to this, then He will give me the strength for it.* She got up and paced, without a limp, eager for her dinner. After eating all that Rosa had prepared for her, she sent a telegram back to the Chief of All Prisons. "Please notify all wardens that Matilda Wrede will again be visiting the prisons."

She began with Kakola Prison, where she had spent so much of her life. She hired a carriage to take her right to the door. In the courtyard, three hundred prisoners greeted her with a song of welcome. When they finished singing, she sat on the chair they offered and they gathered around like school children. Overhead, the sky blazed sunshine and a cool breeze angled down to refresh them.

"No one ever came up Kakola Hill with such thanksgiving in his heart as I just did," she addressed them. "I feel stronger already and my heart is bursting with joy. As long as my strength lasts, I will work for you and your families. I'm so glad to be back."

She talked to them, lectured, and scolded a little, as she had always done. They laughed at her sharp wit. Finally, the tears came and she was obliged to stop.

One prisoner stepped forward and filled her arms with flowers. Four prisoners lifted her chair shoulder-high and carried her in honor to the prison.

Back at Matilda's apartment, Rosa sat in the sunny window seat and copied Matilda's words into the front page of her own Bible. Words which burned in her mind. Words she knew would change her life:

"A life placed in the hands of God will surely be used by Him."

ADDENDUM

Matilda Augusta Wrede was born in Vasa, Finland, on March 8, 1864. She died in Helsinki on December 12, 1928, and was buried in the family vault of the little red stone church in Anjala, near her ancestral home.

The prisoners of Kakola Prison built a statue in her memory. It is located near her grave, which is one of Anjala's attractions.

Her books, family jewelry, gifts from prisoners, and the white convict-made furniture are on display in the Museum of Anjala.

Thanks to her life's work among prisoners, and the efforts of other likeminded persons, prison reform began in Finland, and conditions finally improved.

BIBLIOGRAPHY

Gordon, Ernest B. *A Book of Protestant Saints.* Chicago: Moody Press, 1946, 103–111.

Berry, Eric. *The Land and People of Finland.* Philadelphia: Lippincott, 1972.

Ciszek, Walter and Daniel L. Flaherty. *With God in Russia.* New York: McGraw-Hill Book Company, 1964.

The Finnish-American Reporter (newspaper) Superior, Wisconsin.

Kallos, Hillar and Sylvie Nickels. *Finland: Creation & Construction.* New York: Praeger Publication and London: Allen & Unwin, 1968.

Klinge, Matti. *A Brief History of Finland.* Finland: Otava Printing Works, 1922.

Knowlton, Marylee and Sachner, Mark J. eds. *Children of the World: Finland.* Milwaukee: G. Stevens Publisher

Kurjensaari & Lounela, *Helsinki.* Munich: Matti W. Anderman Publications and New York: Doubleday, 1966.

McNair, Sylvia. *Finland.* New York: Children's Press.

Mead, W.R. *Finland.* New York: Praeger Publishing, 1963.

Ojakangas, Beatrice. *Fantastically Finnish: Recipes and Traditions.* Iowa: Penfield Press, 1985.

Stevenson, Lilian. *Mathilda Wrede of Finland.* London: George Allen & Unwin, Ltd., 1925.

Taylor-Wilkie, Doreen, ed., *Finland.* Boston: Houghton Mifflin, 1966.

Tweedie, Mrs. Alec. *Through Finland in Carts.* London: Adam & Charles Black, 1897.

Wilson, W.G. *In Convict Cells: Mathilda Wrede of Finland.* London: Edinburgh House, 1937.

Read More Great Biographical Fiction from Lois Hoadley Dick

Amy Carmichael: Let the Little Children Come

At twenty-eight, Amy Carmichael left for India, with high hopes of spreading the good news of Christ to the Indian people. The year was 1895, and Amy did not know she was about to encounter a practice that would revolutionize her life and ministry.

God richly blessed Amy's efforts and sent more and more of His "jewels" into her care. This is the story of her significant and remarkable work.

ISBN: 0-8024-0433-2, Paperback

Moody Press, a ministry of Moody Bible Institute,
is designed for education, evangelization, and edification.
If we may assist you in knowing more about Christ
and the Christian life, please write us without obligation:
Moody Press, c/o MLM, Chicago, Illinois 60610.